READING THE MOUNTAINS OF HOME

HARVARD UNIVERSITY PRESS

Cambridge, Massachusetts

London, England

Reading the Mountains of Home

JOHN ELDER

First Harvard University Press paperback edition, 1999

Illustrations by Mark Schroder
Design by Marianne Perlak

Pages 248–249 constitute an extension of the copyright page.

Library of Congress Cataloging-in-Publication Data

Elder, John, 1947–
    Reading the mountains of home / John Elder.
        p. cm.
    Includes bibliographical references (p.   ) and index.
    ISBN 0-674-74888-3 (cloth)
    ISBN 0-674-74889-1 (pbk.)
    1. Bristol Region (Vt.)—Description and travel. 2. Bristol
Region (Vt.)—History. 3. Natural history—Vermont—Bristol Region
4. Hiking—Vermont—Bristol Region. 5. Green Mountains (Vt.)—
Description and travel. 6. Elder, John, 1947– . 7. Frost,
Robert, 1874–1963. Directive. I. Title.
F59.B85E43 1998
917.43'5—dc21   97-36194

For Rachel, Matthew, and Caleb

Contents

Directive

Back out of all this now too much for us,
Back in a time made simple by the loss
Of detail, burned, dissolved, and broken off
Like graveyard marble sculpture in the weather,
There is a house that is no more a house
Upon a farm that is no more a farm
And in a town that is no more a town.
The road there, if you'll let a guide direct you
Who only has at heart your getting lost,
May seem as if it should have been a quarry—
Great monolithic knees the former town
Long since gave up pretense of keeping covered.
And there's a story in a book about it:
Besides the wear of iron wagon wheels
The ledges show lines ruled southeast-northwest,
The chisel work of an enormous Glacier
That braced his feet against the Arctic Pole.
You must not mind a certain coolness from him
Still said to haunt this side of Panther Mountain.
Nor need you mind the serial ordeal
Of being watched from forty cellar holes
As if by eye pairs out of forty firkins.
As for the woods' excitement over you
That sends light rustle rushes to their leaves,
Charge that to upstart inexperience.
Where were they all not twenty years ago?
They think too much of having shaded out
A few old pecker-fretted apple trees.
Make yourself up a cheering song of how
Someone's road home from work this once was,
Who may be just ahead of you on foot
Or creaking with a buggy load of grain.

The height of the adventure is the height
Of country where two village cultures faded
Into each other. Both of them are lost.
And if you're lost enough to find yourself
By now, pull in your ladder road behind you
And put a sign up CLOSED to all but me.
Then make yourself at home. The only field
Now left's no bigger than a harness gall.
First there's the children's house of make-believe,
Some shattered dishes underneath a pine,
The playthings in the playhouse of the children.
Weep for what little things could make them glad.
Then for the house that is no more a house,
But only a belilaced cellar hole,
Now slowly closing like a dent in dough.
This was no playhouse but a house in earnest.
Your destination and your destiny's
A brook that was the water of the house,
Cold as a spring as yet so near its source,
Too lofty and original to rage.
(We know the valley streams that when aroused
Will leave their tatters hung on barb and thorn.)
I have kept hidden in the instep arch
Of an old cedar at the waterside
A broken drinking goblet like the Grail
Under a spell so the wrong ones can't find it,
So can't get saved, as Saint Mark says they mustn't.
(I stole the goblet from the children's playhouse.)
Here are your waters and your watering place.
Drink and be whole again beyond confusion.

—Robert Frost, from *Steeple Bush* (1946)

Introduction

✤ Eighteen years ago our family moved to Bristol, Vermont. Since then I have often hiked a rugged spur of the Green Mountains that looms above and defines our village. Geologists call this ridge the Hogback Anticline. It includes South Mountain, on which Bristol Cliffs Wilderness Area is located, and North, or Hogback, Mountain, soaring on the other side of the New Haven River. In my crisscross explorations of these broken and thickly wooded slopes, I've relied upon the parallel guidance of the Forest Service's topographic maps and Robert Frost's great poem "Directive."

Over the latter part of his long life, Frost maintained a home just a few miles down South Mountain from Bristol, in the hamlet of Ripton. "Directive" does more than any other text to illuminate this particular stretch of New England countryside for me. It integrates the narratives of geology, human settlement, and forest succession into a single, ongoing story. Reflecting about this poem has helped me understand how the mountains around our home assumed their present form, as well as what it might mean to identify with such a place on earth. "Directive" opens by inviting a reader up into the heights. This is an invitation I've accepted with gratitude.

Just as "Directive" sheds light on the character and history of the Green Mountains, so too it depends upon the land for its fullest significance. Certain critical theories assert that literature is no more than a self-referential web of words. But I want to declare that Frost's poem both grows from and contributes to the landscape of Vermont, and that its meaning includes the mountains and the families who have lived among them. When human eloquence is attuned to the processes of the land, it can become, as Frost says in "West-Running Brook," "a tribute of the current to the source." For me, reading and rereading "Directive" has been like a reiterated hike up the spines of two mountains running south to north, end to end, through the middle of Bristol. In the same way, each time I turn my boots up those trails, I am swept back into the circulation of Frost's poem. The seasons, boulders, trees, and animals of the Green Mountains deepen its meaning, image by image and line by line.

Though South Mountain and North Mountain once constituted a single, uninterrupted crest, first the glaciers and then the New Haven River intervened. Twenty thousand years ago, a mile-thick wedge of ice advanced into Vermont with the scourings of the North. The centuries of its melting deposited sediments for a plateau on which the village of Bristol stands today. In "Directive," Frost watches the glaciers come and go and waits for them to come again. While waiting, he calmly regards the forest's own flicker of disappearance and return. The landscape's largest cycles thus inform the poet's perspective on the small farms that also have appeared and disappeared among these heights. The forests along our ridge were in fact mostly cleared, midway through the nineteenth century, because of the charcoal kilns and sheep-pasturing that brought in hill-farmers' main supply of cash. But only a few cellar holes and tumbled stone walls now remain, far in the resurgent woods. Frost incorporates this human reversal—of pioneer families who were defeated by the stony soil and abandoned their homesteads—into his comprehensive vision of succession. He suggests deeper possibilities for communion, both with the land and with one another. "Directive" leads a reader into the hard walking of cut-over and reforested slopes, on a perplexing path toward wholeness.

➤➤➤ This book pursues a sequence of hikes, each of which is framed by several lines from "Directive." The first chapter relates an excursion near the southern end of South Mountain, in late September of 1994. Subsequent hikes progress northward, as well as through the seasons, until arriving at mid-summer of 1995 and the conclusion of Frost's poem. Topographic maps for South Mountain and North Mountain precede the two major parts of the book, in order to delineate the rising and falling contours over which the poem has guided me. One of my goals in the narrative of each hike is to describe the features of our family's home landscape concretely, and to evoke what it feels like to be out in these mountains at a particular time of year. I proceed digressively, frequently checking my bearings in the poem and the maps but often in the end bushwhacking across suspect terrain. I have always had a certain tendency to leave the trail, and consequently to get lost. In this regard, too, "Directive" has been my guide. At the poem's heart is a meditation about getting lost enough "to find yourself" in Vermont's surprising woods.

When preparing for this project of hiking through the poem and along the ridge, I did not foresee the deeper losses and disorientation that the year would bring to me. My father died in California just as I was about to begin, and his kindly image accompanied me on the autumn trails. Immediately after his death, my mother had to undergo major surgery from which recovery was slow. Here in Vermont, one of our children swerved into a phase of adolescence that cut off communication and left our family frightened and confused. In a season such as this, loss among the mountains changed from a literary theme into an urgent and personal story. Thus, although "Directive" enters into each of my chapters, another aspect of the book's continuity has turned out to be its familial narrative. This was not a story I expected to write, but it turned out to be the one that my year brought, that the land accommodated, and that the poem helped me start to shape.

Frost's poem looks past personal losses, though, and moves beyond offering guidance for an individual trying to make a home on earth and raise a family amid the reversals of a life. It also addresses the meaning of loss and recovery for entire communities in this dynamic, challenging landscape. Near the middle of "Directive," we read that "The height of the adventure is the height / Of country where two village cultures faded / Into each other. Both of them are lost." The history of our state reveals, with unique and dramatic clarity, that wilderness can encroach upon civilization as well as the other way around.

In the West, where I grew up and where so many tenets of the environmental movement originated, wilderness has been viewed as a diminishing resource, constantly pushed back by the tide of human settlement. But northern New England is far wilder today than it was a century and a half ago. We've gone from being almost three-quarters cleared to being more than three-quarters forested since the mountains were depopulated. Moose and bear once again thrive on the ridge above our house in Bristol. Such dramatic recoveries within a long-settled landscape make it possible to rethink the relationship between nature and culture in less polarized terms. We have come to a moment, as the conservation movement searches for a more inclusive vision, when the land and history of Vermont have a crucial word to say to the rest of our nation.

⫸ This book's narrative structure and voice differentiate it from literary criticism in the usual sense of the term. Its extended discussions of poetry set it apart from most nature writing. Nor do I pretend to give a comprehensive overview of Frost's achievements as a poet, or even a thorough treatment of the extraordinarily rich poem with which the book's chapters are framed. Rather, my goal has been to explore, in a direct and personal way, an ecosystem of meaning that includes both literature and the land. What a reader will find here are thus the stories of one year's excursions through the mountains where a beloved poem is rooted, and where my family and I also live. Frost's own themes of retreat, loss, recovery, community, and communion have connected the chapters into a unified progression. But since these outings each begin with a new line in the poem and at different coordinates on the map, they also shift continuously with the slopes and outcroppings of an ever-varying topography.

At some points, the discussion thus becomes more absorbed in the poetry itself, while, at others, aspects of natural or familial history dominate. I offer these diverse experiments in outdoor reading in a spirit of friendly conversation with other readers, writers, teachers, and householders pursuing wholeness within their own landscapes. And I remember, in hiking through the terrain of "Directive," that any meanings I may glimpse are inescapably contingent.

SOUTH MOUNTAIN

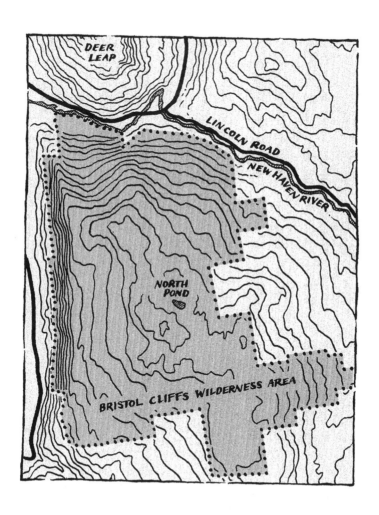

A Wilderness of Scars

> Back out of all this now too much for us,
> Back in a time made simple by the loss
> Of detail, burned, dissolved, and broken off
> Like graveyard marble sculpture in the weather,
> There is a house that is no more a house
> Upon a farm that is no more a farm
> And in a town that is no more a town.

Scars blaze a path into this wilderness. Gray, barkless patches line the edges of my trail, facing inward from the trunks of maples and beech. They mark where log trucks and skidders once scraped their way into the woods. Beanpole popples now crowd the right-of-way, stiff leaves spangling in the lightest breeze. Though over twelve feet high, these pioneers are still yellow-green and smooth. They rise together thickly like a plantation of grass, bend together like stems of grass whenever the forest draws slow breath. Even with weaving in and out among the popples I find the going much easier on this ghost-road than it would be just a few feet to either side. The loggers drove along the natural terracing of the slope, steering around the outcrops and erratics that punctuate the syntax of the forest. Walking on this vestigial track, I also avoid the shattered trunks and fallen branches that elsewhere tilt together into barricades. So I always keep my eye out for the scars.

Bristol Cliffs Wilderness Area was established under the Eastern Wild Areas Act of 1974. But this road had fallen out of use long before that year. The terrain was simply too rugged to repay the mechanized techniques of modern logging. Just below the sign announcing the official boundary of the wilderness, where the slope suddenly tilts steeply upward and boulders arch through the soil on every side like the backs of sounding whales, the blazes disappear. I must keep on moving forward now, in the faith that I will find a large charred stump.

This stump is a relic, perhaps as much as sixty years old according to our County Forester, David Brynn, of a fire fed by the slash from logging. It rises to a delicate black point, attenuated by the shuttling seasons of rain and snow that have also leached away most of its internal substance. Only a delicate design of wafered carbon remains, radiating from the center of the stump like the secret gills that fan out, invisible from above, around a mushroom's central bole. When I reach this bearing-stump, I turn due east and cast around for my next charcoal monument. There it is, a second stump standing on its own small rise, surrounded by four rocks similar to it in size. From here on, I can orient myself to a slimy ash log that points up the slope and disappears into a burst of jewelweed, its delicate foliage hanging above the ground like blue-green smoke from summer's last explosion in the woods. My boots disappear beneath the jewelweed, so that I stumble on the broken ground. After ascending through this confusion, though, I return to the more sustained instruction of a trail.

In fact, the going is now even clearer than on the old logging road below. Ted Lylis, whose property is just to the south of here on Lower Notch Road, told me that this higher trail was part of a track constructed in the mid-nineteenth century. Long before motorized skidders plied the lower woods, it was the path for bringing teams of oxen into the heights. Extensive leveling was necessary to bend a sturdy dogleg trail from Bristol Flats up to the talus-spilling brow of Bristol Cliffs. In the intervening years, though the way has narrowed

to a footpath, the walking has remained firm on black earth packed in the crevices between cobbles. Where the trail, which has been climbing northeast until now, ricochets sharply to the south, an iron cable dangles down, one end embedded deep in the trunk of an ancient birch. It was originally placed here so that ox-drivers could run the cable through the harness of their animals. That way, as Ted said to me, if the animals did lose their footing in trying to drag a load around this cornice, "they still wouldn't end up at the bottom as tenderized beef."

When I finally make it to the top, a raddled plateau rising toward the town of Lincoln, I still see traces of long-vanished human livelihoods. Stone walls stalk through the trees, marking the pastures where sheep were put to graze after the first great deforestation. Trees growing here when the European settlers arrived were often cut not so much to clear farmland or provide lumber as to feed the kilns that produced charcoal for the iron furnaces and forges of Bristol, Monkton, and Vergennes. One major kiln operated near this trail, producing charcoal for the bloomery furnaces just below.

Bristol Cliffs Wilderness Area could certainly not be described as "vast," "untrammeled," or "pristine"—the defining adjectives from the 1964 Wilderness Act. The thick woods that frame the Cliffs today are not even *second*-growth. They are the third distinct forest community to flourish here since the Wisconsin Glacier melted around 12,000 years ago. This arboreal succession mirrors a larger pattern of constant and momentous change in the local landscape, beginning long before immigrants from Massachusetts and New York established themselves here. The first big development of our present interglacial period, after the ice had scraped Bristol Cliffs down to its resistant bedrock of Cheshire quartzite, came when subarctic species like the spruces and willows repioneered the slopes. They were followed, as the climate warmed, by southerly species like beech and maple, chestnut, hickory, and oak. Wilderness here has always been a vector, never a steady state.

Enormous mammals wandered through the newly opened land—giant buffalo and beaver, woolly mammoths, dire wolves, and short-faced bears. But as paths thawed through the Canadian ice-shield, allowing paleolithic hunters to penetrate southward from the Siberian landbridge, these stupendous creatures began to disappear. Fossil records indicate that they were extinct in most areas of North and South America within half a century of humans' first arrival in a given locale—just about the same span of time it later took the European settlers to shear away the forests from these slopes. While various explanations have been offered, many researchers now believe that those first people in America killed the largest denizens of their new home faster than they could eat their prey. Who needs to finish butchering or to cure old meat when there is an endless fresh supply? This account suggests that "Food" was a dream of perfect plenty for these early Vermont hunters, like "Iron" or "Land" for their booted, ax-handling successors. How, I wonder, could newcomers have avoided such fantasies, arriving without the stories, fitted to this place, that might have made them feel at home? But the stories of home do come, arising through misapprehension and disaster, and also through unforeseen connections between our individual lives, our communities, and the grandeur of the land.

The deforestation and eradications carried out in their turn by European settlers were pretty much complete by the time Zadock Thompson wrote *The Natural History of Vermont* in 1854. His survey recorded that mountain lions and wolves had long vanished. Even our scaled-down beaver and white-faced deer, both so plentiful in Vermont today, were then extinct in much of the state. Within the economic sphere as well as in the realm of biology, impoverishment seemed the Green Mountains' destiny. The early iron mines had not produced a pure enough grade of ore to compete with the diggings on the western side of Lake Champlain—operations which had the added advantage of being closer to the canals and other new commercial routes. The boom in merino sheep soon turned into a bust as well, as the western states and Australia established much vaster and more profitable operations.

Between the Revolution and the Civil War, Vermont had been the fastest growing state in the Union, and the early entrepreneurs had established enough mills and forges along the rivers, enough limestone and charcoal kilns in the mountains, to place Vermont at the forefront of the industrial revolution. With the Civil War, however, came one of the dramatic reversals that bend through Vermont's history like the doglegs of a rugged mountain trail. For most of the next century, it was the slowest growing state. Whole communities of hill-farmers headed out for the newly opened Midwest, eager to sail their plows over the heartland's topsoil after years spent navigating the shoals of these glaciated highlands. But such human failures and departures also heralded a strong comeback for the forests, in this wet land so good at growing trees.

A complete cycle of reforestation has been accomplished twice within the modern period. After the merinos lit out for the territories, white pines crowded into their abandoned pastures. They thrived in the full sun and readily germinated in the grassy carpet that had so recently been pasture for sheep. Once these pioneers shaded the ground with a dark new canopy, few white pine seedlings were able to sprout. But the existing ones continued to rise in lofty groves until, around the turn of the present century, Vermont's loggers too arose in force to harvest the bonus crop of prime softwood. For several decades, there was a thriving settlement about a mile and a half south of here in Bristol Notch, inhabited by the families of sawyers and millhands. Large-scale logging was pretty much played out near Bristol Cliffs by 1925, however. At that point some of the houses in the Notch were sold for deer camps, while others simply subsided into the forest floor.

The present forest of mixed northern hardwoods has developed largely since the 1920s. While spruce, fir, and birch dominate above 2500 feet in the Green Mountains, these mountains are also now stocked with beech, oak, hickory, butternut, white pine, red pine, hemlock, and, most notably each fall, with multitudes of maples. Durable kernels from the deciduous trees bided their time for years in a buried seed pool, ready to burst upward from the ground exposed and torn by logging. The autumnal vividness that saturates the sky above me now is thus the offspring of two eradicated forests.

One reason South Mountain's sugar maple leaves have turned so astonishingly *red,* here at the end of September, is that they have suddenly become bereft of *green.* As the days have shortened and cooled, the maples have cut off the supply of precious nitrogen to their extremities, arresting photosynthesis and, with it, the production of chlorophyll. A sharp withdrawal of nitrogen scratches the match that annually ignites these mountains. Summer flares up in a vivid combustion, before drifting down in embers through the branches' bare gray mesh. The circle of the year turns, and is illuminated, in the transient glow of leaves. Over the coming weeks, as the Canada geese and snow geese pass southward, morning and evening, through our lives, their calls will float down with those changing leaves. Familiar cycles of departure offer those of us who stay a way to feel at home.

> Back out of all this now too much for us,
> Back in a time made simple by the loss
> Of detail . . .

The first lines of "Directive" call a reader to attention like two cracks of a whip. "Back out of all this now too much for us" also expresses an impulse to retreat, to find an escape from the pressures of modern life. The need for such respite has certainly not lessened since the poem was published in 1946. On a recent Sunday afternoon, I was out jogging on Plank Road near Bristol. Beyond the road-hugging cornfields rose glowing views of the Green Mountains to the east and the Adirondacks to the west. A Volvo station wagon suddenly crested the hill beside a sentinel oak, spinning a cloud of dust behind it. Within was a man driving with one hand on the wheel and the other clutching a cellular telephone. His brow was furrowed and his eyes, glimpsed through the windshield as he sped past, looked blind to the season. "Too much for us"—the world of goals, responsibilities, and social identity. This line echoes a sonnet by Wordsworth, Frost's favorite poet, that begins:

> The world is too much with us; late and soon.
> Getting and spending, we lay waste our powers.
> Little we see in nature that is ours . . .

We become so distracted by our own agendas that, even when face to face with the grandeur of nature, we can only exclaim with Wordsworth, "Great God! It moves us not." Though I had no cellular phone with me on the run, I identified with the worried-looking driver. I too found my vision continually blurred by fretting about assignments, my head crammed with all the tasks looming with Monday and the new week.

If "all this now" stands for the overwhelming present, Frost's next line reinforces the poem's *pastoral* impulse—to recover "a time made simple by the loss / Of detail." We want to back up because, in retrospect at least, the past seems simpler; we want to find some place that represents or has preserved that past. Looking backward at our rural history, though, we may forget the oppressive labor of moving through unfamiliar mountains as a family or of making a new life together in the wilderness. Nostalgia, like other forms of sentimentality, can be an isolating fantasy, a barrier between us and the true objects of our desire.

The verbs that follow in Frost's poem shred the gauzy longing for "a time made simple." He describes such a loss of definition as ". . . burned, dissolved, and broken off / Like graveyard marble sculpture in the weather." Pastoral longing can be a form of oblivion, even an erasure, like the elements' blurring of inscriptions in a New England graveyard. This is an arresting image for the losses that made the past, too, an overwhelming "now" for our ancestors in Vermont. I've peered at the names and dates of the old stones in a Quaker cemetery, just up the road from Bristol in South Starksboro. In a single winter, many children in that community, including all three in one family, were carried off by influenza. When these already faint inscriptions are further eroded by the rain, the cracking stones even more blotched by lichen, that winter will recede from clarity behind the perpetually fluffy snowfall of a New England paperweight Christmas. But Frost will not allow such forgetting in his poem. His exuberant opening sags by the fourth line into a litany of two-syllable words, made listless by the fact that in each case the second syllable is unstressed—"graveyard," "marble," "sculpture," "weather."

Dramatic shifts of tone like this one occur throughout the poem, giving it an unpredictable quality, like that of my present footing in these woods. No frost has yet withered the bracken, sensitive ferns, woodferns, jewelweed, nettles, or other small herbaceous plants that make this ground look more level than it actually is. But in reality stones break through the soil on all sides and migrate downhill year by year, so that I'm constantly stumbling against a chunk of quartzite or lurching into the low spot where one used to be. Both in reading "Directive" and in hiking here, I have to slow down and take it step by step, and often have to turn aside from my anticipated line. Advancing through such a landscape, I meet the rocky particularity of a world below the eye's first easy, green impression.

The fifth through seventh lines of the poem are notable, after the beginning's gustiness, for the regularity of their rhythm. Their iambic steadiness is reinforced by the fact that every word is a single syllable and each of the lines reflects the same simple syntax:

> There is a house that is no more a house
> Upon a farm that is no more a farm
> And in a town that is no more a town.

This repetitive simplicity is like a riddle. When *is* a house no more a house, a farm no more a farm, a town no more a town? Answering such a question requires hiking further up into the paradoxical wilderness of Vermont. In the course of "Directive" we will indeed come to a house, deep in the woods, that is now no more than a cellar hole, to a farm that has vanished except for its last vestigial clearing. Where there was once a town of hard-working families along the ridge, we will enter a thickening forest that might seem at first sight never to have been inhabited by humans. The answer to the poem's conundrums is in fact the land itself, with its history still inscribed in the processes of its present.

Frost's opening lines not only point up to the ridge above Bristol, they also identify a tension fundamental to America's environmental movement. We long to save wild beauty from heedless development, to guarantee a modicum of biodiversity in the world of internal combustion engines and electronic monoculture. Within the wilderness ethic, as in the poem's first line, there is an impulse to get *back,* to recover an understanding that the natural world has integrity and value beyond our human enterprises. We need to remember, as Gary Snyder has expressed it, that the earth is more than "a vast supply depot" on which to draw as we work out our heavenly destiny here below. In this regard, wilderness possesses great spiritual value. It offers a realm for human activity that does not seek to take possession and that leaves no traces; it provides a baseline for strenuous experience of our own creaturehood.

When my wife Rita and I take the family camping, clean water becomes once more the most precious substance in the world, rather than the invisible, untasted current flowing through our taps. We feel our legs at the end of a day on the trail, and are grateful for a level place to bed down that night, for a warm bag and a tent or tarp to keep us dry. These basic pleasures are exhilarating by contrast with the technological complexity and overload of "all this now too much for us." Leaving behind homes, schools, jobs, cars, newspapers, television, radio, CDs (both kinds), sojourners in the mountains enter "a world made simple by the loss of detail." We even leave behind the realm of money since, as Bill McKibben says, there is nothing to buy five miles into the woods.

But there is a pointed warning in the connection that "Directive" draws between such a simplifying impulse and a scouring away of historical details. In affirming wilderness both as a physical area protected under law and as a source of renewal for individuals, we need to be aware of how easily we can fall into a false dichotomy. One reason Native American people so often criticize the language of wilderness is that it seems to be defined in opposition to the human realm—as wilderness versus culture, or as land devoid of human settlements. They see this as a tourist's admiration for "nature," in contrast with their own experience of living in daily communion with a nonhuman world that contains a multitude of persons, akin to us in many important ways and possessing their own spirits and destinies.

"Directive" does not explicitly address the American wilderness movement. Nor does Frost make any reference in it to the indigenous cultures of his New England home. But, at the very beginning of his remarkable poem, he both acknowledges the desire for release from our oppressive present and warns against a nostalgia that would close our eyes to everything but an undifferentiated pastoral blur. The three riddling lines quoted earlier provoke a reader to ask what kind of place this really *is*, and to discover what history culminates in such a landscape. Answering these questions requires a deeper foray into the thickening forests of Vermont. "Directive" is the map for such an excursion. It is the poem of eastern wilderness.

➤ The Eastern Wilderness Act of 1974 sought to acknowledge and protect pockets of recovered wildness like Bristol Cliffs, one of the first two wildernesses designated in Vermont under the new act. Precisely because this is no pristine expanse on the western model, we can perhaps learn to appreciate it even more as a *providential* one. Relics germinate in the forest floor, and an inadvertent beauty rises through abandonment.

In the vast wildernesses of the West, such as Glacier National Park or Gates of the Arctic, one can readily leave behind all sight or sound of other humans, wandering into roadless areas with no visible record of past settlements. But Bristol Cliffs, though protected by a similar congressional mandate, is only 3,740 acres in all. Walking up this trail beneath the cliffs, I can still hear the heavy rigs bowling up Route 7 and the chainsaws whining and sputtering in woodlots just off Notch Road. Tumbledown stone walls run from one side of the wilderness to the other. Majestic stumps are bedded damply amid dark green star-moss and emerald sphagnum. Such relics insist that this wilderness is no stable phenomenon beyond the human grasp but, rather, a bundle of stories. History, of course, essentially means a story, and "Directive" has helped me to see the human and natural history of Bristol Cliffs as *one*. The import of this tattered little scrap of eastern wilderness is far-reaching. It shows that wilderness can grow as well as shrink. But it can never stay the same, and people are included in its living web.

I've often pored over the topographic maps for Bristol Cliffs, trying to memorize the features of this bewilderingly intricate terrain. The green shape of the wilderness area itself, as identified on the Forest Service map, suggests a rather untidy patchwork quilt. With its irregular margins (and one little square is even shorn away from wilderness within the interior of the collage) this assemblage of smaller tracts proclaims a painstakingly negotiated accommodation for wilderness within the dominant realm of surveyors and real estate. "Wilderness Boundary" is printed over and over in the gray band marking the protected area's edge. In contrast to much of western wilderness, then, Bristol Cliffs is a landscape where it is impossible to forget the prevalence of edges—edges between private land and federally designated wilderness, but also between human history and the rest of nature.

Ecologists speak of the meeting between two ecosystems as an "ecotone," partaking of some of the physical attributes of each constituent environment and harboring some of the creatures from each as well. Within such a meeting ground, "edge-effect" prevails, in a diversity of species that exceeds those of the separate ecosystems as well as in the relative density of individual organisms. An edge is a risky opportunity. It offers new sources of food for creatures venturing out from the fundamental safety of familiar ground, but also exposes them as potential sources of nourishment for fellow opportunists creeping in from the opposite side.

The light green composite patched together on the topo map represents a remarkable return of wildness in our town. As the logging roads fade, game trails proliferate. Circumambulating the boggy mountaintop jewel called North Pond, I have seen and followed enormous moose prints in the mud and passed huge areas where moose had crumpled the bracken flat to snooze through a September night. Bear prints sometimes linger in the soft black agar, too, and clawmarks are scored deeply into the rinds of certain beeches. A month ago, in August, while crossing an upland meadow laden with blueberries, and not more than half a mile from here, I passed a decisive line beyond which bears had exercised their considerable patience and expertise to remove every last berry from among the leathery leaves. The standing snags of this abandoned timber yard also nourish pileated woodpeckers who can disclose a book-sized cavity in the corky deadwood within a single afternoon of flying chips. All day a tenured faculty of corvids shout across the pond, blessedly unintelligible to me, at least, while at night owls float forth in silent speculation.

John Muir, as much as he admired Thoreau (propping his picture on the mantel of his Martinez ranch house), mocked his Massachusetts forerunner's sense that there could be anything wild in the huckleberry and puckerbrush thickets around Concord. For Thoreau's famous dictum from the essay "Walking"—"In wildness is the preservation of the world"—Muir substituted his own formulation—"In God's wilderness is the preservation of the world." Muir's life and writing inspired the western wilderness movement, with its orientation to sublime religious visions in mountains so much loftier and more monolithic than these rounded, tree-wrapped ridges. He strongly influenced our current association between wildness and tremendous expanses of wilderness.

But Frost, for whom Wordsworth and Thoreau, and before them Virgil, were the chosen ancestors, values wildness at the *edge* and even in the *midst* of civilization; he sees it not as a factor of extent or separation, but rather as a quality of mindful attentiveness promoted by vivid, sensually impressive contrasts. Thoreau loved the wetlands and other "unproductive" areas not apart from but in relation to the cultivated lands, as revitalizing elements for entire regions. Growing up in the Bay Area, I relished occasional car trips into the vastness and beauty of the Sierra Nevada. But as a householder in Vermont, I love even more the tattered, recovering wilderness just outside our back door, where in every season our family can ramble among the crags that overhang our roof and that frame the playing fields of the children's schools.

≫ The topo map I hold in my hand almost comically reflects the intricate brokenness of Bristol Cliffs. Contour lines radiate outward and downward from the high point (2,325 feet) just above North Pond. But, rather than registering smooth concentrics, the lines take on the extreme irregularity of ripples in a mountain kettle-hole, which must fan out across a surface constantly pierced by rocks, stumps, and the rigid stems of sedge. Implicated lines lean out around each interrupting point, then snap back to the next obstacle around the edge. Similarly, for a hiker *in* the map, this bouldery glacial scour impedes the straightforward, peak-grabbing stride invited by the often broad and level trails of western wilderness. Stumbling through gullies in Vermont, I don't always know which way leads on toward the ridge. Sometimes, the best course is just to stop and admire the unmapped beauty of riven boulders set amid the woodferns.

Brown contour lines shadow the map's pale green like an etcher's fine cross-hatching, in depicting how the cliffs from which the wilderness area gets its name rise 1200 feet in less than half a mile. But even this dramatic upward thrust yields to constant distractions. It flickers past secret dripping swales, lifts by ledges broad as dance floors, stumbles where talus brusquely sweeps away the trees. Like Frost's verse, with its underlying iambic tendency, there is a general vector here—*upward,* left boot, right boot, toward the heights. As in reading the poet's masterful, fissured lines, though, I also find my forward motion constantly deflected in Bristol Cliffs, as I slide down a sudden drop-off or scrabble with hands and feet up a root-bound rock face. Dante distinguished between poetry that is neatly combed *(pexa)* and a shaggier, unkempt thicket of rhythms and sounds *(hirsuta).* The same categories might be applied to land. The amplitude of Bristol Cliffs Wilderness comes neither from spatial extensiveness nor from the lofty canopy and parklike floor of eastern old-growth. It comes instead from bad footing in a shaggy, third-growth forest within walking distance of the homes in Bristol village.

Planners in the public forests of the West have taken pains to preserve a "beauty strip" along highways and scenic rivers, a wall of trees obscuring the rapacity of clear-cuts that flay the earth for mile after mile behind that fringe. From an airplane closing in on Portland or Seattle, though, the devastation is exposed. Those forests are like the green border of a patchwork quilt from which the lovingly quilted center has been scissored away square by square. Bristol Cliffs Wilderness is the inverse. It only touches the road briefly in the gap where Route 116 parallels the New Haven River and again for a few hundred yards along Briggs Hill Road in Lincoln. There is no direct access to the wilderness area from the south or on the side below the western cliffs. I can only gain the log road that whispers faintly upward to the old ox-path by first marching up a long driveway and asking permission of the landowner, Mrs. Kilbourne, to cross her back lot.

Looking upward from the log cabins and ranch houses of Notch Road, a newcomer to Bristol might suppose that everything in these mountains was already parceled out and sellable. The dynamic ruggedness and the federally protected status of the wilderness area would come as a surprise if that visitor then climbed up and penetrated the fringe of settlement. Just so, someone who looks down from a small plane crossing almost any part of northern New England or the Adirondacks is struck by the dark forests that absolutely dominate this entire region of the country, divided only occasionally by strips of settlement along a road or river. Wildness is deeply rooted in our region, and our towns are grounded, surrounded, and sustained by it.

If the topo map is like an overflight, Frost's "Directive," narrating a hike up this wilderness ridge, offers a different kind of guidance. Finding our human place in the wilderness with the help of a *story-map* accords with traditional Native American preferences to integrate the human and the natural. The Laguna Pueblo novelist Leslie Marmon Silko has written an essay called "Landscape, History, and the Pueblo Imagination" in which she explores this connection with reference to the traditions of her own people. In the essay's third section, "Through the Stories We Hear Who We Are," she notes that

a dinner table conversation, recalling a deer hunt forty years ago, inevitably stimulates similar memories in listeners. But hunting-stories were not merely after-dinner entertainment. These accounts contained information of critical importance about behavior and migration patterns of mule deer. Hunting stories carefully described key landmarks and locations of fresh water. Thus a deer-hunt story might also serve as a "map." Lost travelers, and lost piñon-nut gatherers, have been saved by sighting a rock formation they recognize only because they once heard a hunting story describing this rock formation.

How, though, may individuals who do not live in a rooted, indigenous culture, and who do not participate in the living exchange of hunting stories, attain the vital orientation of such a story-map?

For me, "Directive" has offered one way to make a start. In part, this is because it conveys the natural and human stories of the mountains around Bristol, this village where Rita and I are raising our family. As Gary Snyder has written in *The Practice of the Wild*, a culture, and an individual, may become more fully integrated through close, sustained identification with one particular bioregion. He contrasts such unity of culture and nature with "the insubstantial world of political jurisdictions and rarefied economies"—in short, with Frost's modern world of "all this now too much for us." Finding ourselves thus also requires for Snyder "discovering the original lineaments of our land." And literature specific to our place may have a special power to connect us, akin to the power of stories in an oral tradition. I am not an Abenaki. Nor would I be considered a Vermonter, having grown up largely in northern California and come east only for graduate school. Even my children, though born here, would not be called Vermonters by most members of long-time Bristol families. (My neighbors might well respond, if I put the question to them, with the old Vermont joke: "If the cat has kittens in the oven, does that make them biscuits?") But if not "native," I can still aspire to the kind of close relation with the land that Snyder calls "inhabitory." This will call on me to pay attention to the stories of the land, and of the previous generations who lived and died among these reforested hills.

Hiking a poem and reading a wilderness, like cultivating a relationship with the land, can never be passive experiences. They require creative participation. Silko reveals that the Pueblo stories so essential to her people's survival are no more monolithic or static than the woods of Bristol Cliffs Wilderness Area.

> Communal storytelling was a self-correcting process in which listeners were encouraged to speak up if they noted an important fact or detail omitted . . . Implicit in the Pueblo oral tradition was the awareness that loyalties, grudges, and kinship must always influence the narrator's choices as she emphasizes to listeners that this is the way *she* has always heard the story told. The ancient Pueblo people sought a communal truth, not an absolute. For them this truth lived somewhere within the web of differing versions.

The hikes that compose this book are my own partial, and necessarily biased, versions of the woods, and of Frost's poem. Out of the openings and limitations of my own experience, I offer this contribution to what Silko calls the "ancient continuous story composed of innumerable bundles of other stories."

I feel a new urgency to become rooted and at home in these mountains above Bristol. A month ago, on August 19, 1994, my father died in California. My brother Lyn and I scattered his ashes in a grove of laurel and redwood trees on Tamalpais, the mountain rising just to the north of our boyhood home. Dad's death has left me feeling unmoored in the world. He always seemed the wise sponsor of my own adulthood. With Lyn's permission I reserved a small bag of the ashes to bring back to Vermont, wanting to seed them into our family's chosen homeland in New England. I've been hiking every day with these ashes in my pack, looking for the right monument of stone, tree, or water by which to bestow Dad's remains, as a landmark for our family's future life together here. When I discover a fitting spot, I'll make an entry in my journal and draw a little map, so that in later years Rachel, Matthew, and Caleb might find their own way to the place where maple leaves or woodferns unfold our familial history beneath the sky of Bristol Cliffs.

Twilight has overtaken me on this afternoon's excursions along the edge of wilderness. Each evening, at this time of year, as light fades overhead, the foliage seems for a few moments to glow even more brightly. Walking back down the trail before the shadowed footing becomes too treacherous, I come to a mature sugar maple of remarkable beauty. This tree is standing alone on a last wrinkle of high ground before my descent to Mrs. Kilbourne's drive, its crown rounded into the broad, unmistakable contour of the species. Its trunk, luminous with the reflected glory of the maple's top, records a world of interwoven lives. The bark is a rugged amalgam of gray and tan, with corky segments curling outward almost like hickory bark. Occasionally, a stripe of bare wood is exposed, showing long thin cracks like those in ice-tried granite, but not yet with any of those little wasp borings that presage the arrival of woodpeckers and spell the beginning of the end. Crevices in the bark do abound with lichen and moss, though. A pale green lichen grows all over the tree—a rubbery compound of clustering oval leaves that look like tiny lettuce. Pinkish lichen, of a finer, almost powdery texture, is splotched more sparsely up the trunk. Each lichen is a symbiosis, with an alga photosynthetically producing food and a fungus providing structural support for the nourishing alchemy of its partner's perpetual decay. As these pink and green collaborations swirl in eddies up the trunk, moss wells from the deeper pockets like bubbles spilled from a retreating wave.

I turn and follow the tide of light back down the slope, making my way home through the wilderness along a trail of all that has been lost.

Hiking by Flashlight

LOST AT NIGHT
OCTOBER 10, 1994

> The road there, if you'll let a guide direct you
> Who only has at heart your getting lost,
> May seem as if it should have been a quarry—
> Great monolithic knees the former town
> Long since gave up pretense of keeping covered.

Not long after I came to Middlebury College in 1973, I found myself seated next to Victor Reichert at a dinner. Rabbi Reichert, who both taught at a seminary and served a congregation in Cincinnati, had summered in Ripton for many years and was a close friend of Robert Frost. With his mane of white hair and his personal gravity, he reminded me of the poet with whom he had long delighted in discussing the Bible. In an attempt to get a conversation started with this impressive man, I remarked that I too was a great admirer of Frost's work, especially of the poem "Directive." Rabbi Reichert slowly turned his gaze toward me and in a gentle voice commanded, "Say it." I can recall my first moment of blank terror, after which I began to babble "Back out of all this now too much for us, / Back . . ." "All right," he said, and with a little smile passed me the rolls.

Like the rabbi, Frost enjoys putting his reader on the spot. Beyond his pleasure in the humor that comes with abruptly raising the stakes, he has a serious desire to get past formalities and abstractions, right to the essentials. The first seven lines of "Directive" lay out the themes and questions that the poem will pursue, but then comes a change to the concrete and personal. This is the point where I always feel that startled, visceral *engagement* in the poem that was also produced by Victor Reichert's gambit.

> The road there, if you'll let a guide direct you
> Who only has at heart your getting lost,
> May seem as if it should have been a quarry—

The sudden address to "you" gives the poem a more directly personal quality. Having hooked me—with the opening's compelling rhythms, its reference to my desire for escape from an overwhelming world, and its riddle about house, farm, and town—the "guide" now allows himself to take liberties. Even with the unanticipated intimacy of this voice, the intentions of the speaker are not always clear. I begin to suspect that he is keeping secrets from me even while counseling about my next move. When he confides that he "only has at heart your getting lost," I catch a whiff of sarcasm in his Yankee dryness. What sort of guide is *that* to trust? As in the dinner conversation with Rabbi Reichert, there is an edge of danger in these friendly words.

Like Dante at the beginning of the *Inferno,* this guide invites the reader of "Directive" into dark, confusing woods "che la diritta via era smarrita"—"where the straight way was lost." Both works sweep up a reader who is "nel mezzo del cammin di nostra vita"—one who is overwhelmed by the losses, anxiety, and bewilderment here "in the middle of our life's journey." They both start a reader like me on a walking meditation in which my own sense of urgency will magnify the sights along the way. It might seem disproportionate to compare the first of Dante's grand *cantiche* with a twentieth-century poem of fewer than a hundred lines. But I believe it is impossible to overestimate the ambition of this, Frost's most difficult poem, which will finish after all with communion and the Grail.

"Directive"'s personal address to the reader coincides with a much more regular rhythm than that of its opening several lines. This steadier cadence also goes along with the poem's first concrete and specific images of the landscape. Frost is moving into a precise, and significant, description of Vermont's terrain. The early hill-farmers' attempts at road grading often had an even shorter life than their farms, gullying away in the freshets of April snow-melt. Even today, when the town trucks spread mountains of dirt and gravel every year, the road from Lincoln to Ripton can be a jaw-rattling encounter with ledges and outcrops disguised by the thinnest coat of dust. Beyond the wonders of annual erosion in the Green Mountains, this is a land where, each winter, boulders pop out of the soil like corks, propelled upward by the inexorable frost. A hike on the nearby Long Trail, where it crosses over Mt. Abraham, can at times resemble rock climbing more than walking.

With all his sympathy for the efforts of those who tried to farm these mountains, Frost never forgets that geology is destiny. Looking at the USDA *Soil Survey of Addison County,* one can see why the ridge above our home was abandoned in the first place, allowing it to grow wild for this moment. The fat alluvial soils of prosperous dairy farms to our west, near Lake Champlain, are identified on the survey maps by codes such as *Cw* and *VgB*—"Covington and Panton silty clays" and "Vergennes clay, 2 to 6 percent slopes." By contrast, the land around Bristol Cliffs is scarified by labels like *LxE*—"Lyman-Berkshire very rocky complex, 20 to 50 percent slopes"—or simply *Rk.* Frost's rueful tone is appropriate when contemplating the lot of those who set out to homestead in such a bony tract.

"Quarry" is one of those words in "Directive" to which a special emphasis has been given, by wedging it into the fault, or edge, between the two halves of Frost's long second sentence. It describes the blocky, hewn look of exposed rock in this region. The New Haven River assumes the aspect of a staircase when it runs through

Bristol, descending over a series of sharply differentiated stone ter-races and steps. The word also promises some *product* from the la-bor of hiking and reading. It remains to be seen at this point whether this will be iron-ore or limestone, such as early settlers found in Bristol, or gravel, such as is dredged out of quarries around our town today. It's also possible that there is more precious metal to be mined here—not so long ago, men dug for silver in these hills. Finally, "quarry" suggests the hunt, with a stag pursued into thick cover. Soon after this point in the poem, animals do emerge, haunt-ing the mountain and peering out of holes. Lost in dark woods and with an untrustworthy guide, I start to wonder just who the quarry might turn out to be.

There is certainly a hint of mockery in the line "Who only has at heart your getting lost"—a teasing mildness about a scary proposi-tion. At the same time, the poem as a whole shows how *earnest* this apparently wayward intention is. James Joyce's word "jocoserious," from *Ulysses,* might be a good one for describing this complex tone. The next two lines, too, have an intriguing and humorous effect:

> Great monolithic knees the former town
> Long since gave up pretense of keeping covered.

This mountain has a dress that's just too *short*. It simply doesn't have enough soil to cover its extraordinary rockiness or decently clothe its farms (and farm families). The abandonment of efforts at propriety by the "former town" evokes the Yankee eccentrics who thrive to-day in this ledgy landscape as they did when Frost wrote—old women and old men who do and say just what they like, no longer pretending to maintain a proper decorum. There's a freedom in such relinquishment of forms, in giving up the habit of tugging on a skirt that's not likely, after all, to lengthen for the pulling. It's like the openness to imagination that comes from letting go, and from embracing our place in a history of failure and dislocation through which we may nonetheless find a home. With the reference to

"Great knees," the picture also suddenly contains a *giant,* looking down with (as yet) no comment as a traveler and an untrustworthy guide forge slowly up the slope. Now that the expedition is well under way, the guide's remarks come to seem increasingly gothic and, one half suspects, even malicious.

I come back to that line, "The road there, if you'll let a guide direct you . . ." "If" makes poetry possible for Frost. Not "what if," indicating some world contrary to everything we know; "if" as the act of imagination that roots poetry in the concrete facts of a real, engendering world. Marianne Moore defined poetry as imaginary gardens with real toads in them. But for Frost the garden is real, and imagination is the discipline of registering, as immediately and inclusively as possible, all of the lives and meanings a particular landscape may harbor. His use of "if" as an invitation into the mountains of Vermont also grows out of a tradition of literary mapping. Poets, no less than forests, have a living history. The buried seedpool from which "Directive" grew is Wordsworth's "Michael." Like Frost, Wordsworth fused his spiritual and emotional life with the contours of the land. Like the New England poet's, the English writer's home on earth was a marginal terrain, where human hopes and prosperity often foundered but also where a certain bleak and disrupted quality could foster a deeper understanding of humanity's essential bond with nature.

"Michael" begins,

> If from the public way you turn your steps
> Up the tumultuous brook of Green-head Ghyll,
> You will suppose that with an upright path
> Your feet must struggle; in such bold ascent
> The pastoral mountains front you, face to face.
> But courage! for around that boisterous brook

> The mountains have all opened out themselves,
> And made a hidden valley of their own.

In both "Directive" and "Michael," the poet's work is one of *disclosure*. There is a place in the mountains whose existence one might never suspect, without guidance from one who has been there. And in both cases, the site toward which the reader is led is where a family used to live. For Frost, this is an overgrown farmstead, while for Wordsworth it is the tumbled-down sheepfold of long-vanished shepherds. A hiker in that valley would probably not even recognize the vestige of the sheepfold in "a heap of straggling stones," were it not for the guide who pauses and notes that "to that simple object appertains a story." The life of shepherds among those hills, under that sky, comes alive again in the world of "if."

The summer before last, our family made a pilgrimage to Grasmere. We followed Wordsworth's directions up into "Michael"'s hidden pastoral landscape, walking as he instructed along "the tumultuous brook of Green-head Ghyll." The poem itself is a valley of sympathy, within which old covenants may be restored. We read in it of how the shepherd Michael and his son Luke began making the stone sheepfold together, as a symbol of their mutual bond of love, and of their shared bond to the land. When Luke left, never to return, that covenant might have remained broken and the sheepfold unfinished had it not been for the fortitude of the aged Michael, who labored on faithfully until his death, and for the memory and imagination of a poet whose efforts were

> for the sake
> Of youthful Poets, who among these hills
> Will be my second self when I am gone.

I grew up in northern California, amid hills where I once ran with my dog and flew kites but which are now the fenced domains of gaudy residential fortresses. Where can the wholeness of life be found when the hills of childhood are subdivided? Wordsworth's answer, and Frost's in "Directive," is that by looking closely at what remains, a poet may evoke a wholeness that both includes and depends upon a concrete past. I have a snapshot of our son Matthew soberly laying his own stone on the little pile our family made in the valley of "Michael." The photograph was made right after we had finished reading the poem aloud, under a sky wheeling with hawks and in a treeless upland with only bracken and purple foxglove rising above the grass. We wanted the power of that story to flow into the life of our family.

➤➤➤ I've been poring over the annals of Bristol, searching for stories of how other families led their lives among these rocks, these woods. When Harvey Munsill died in 1876 he left a voluminous manuscript covering both the topography of his hometown and some of the main events in its first century. George III had chartered a township here in 1762, naming it Pocock after one of his admirals. But the French and Indian Wars made this a chancy locale for farming, and the only European settler before the Revolution was apparently a New York fugitive from justice who lived in a cave below the cliffs. The state legislature changed the name from Pocock to Bristol in 1789, and the Munsills and other founding families arrived over the following decade. As an old man in the 1860s, Harvey Munsill began to look back over the progress of the community, assembling lists of all who came to take the Freeman's Oath as citizens of Bristol, names and dates of the three churches' ministers, chronicles of the rise and fall of forges, kilns, and mills, and a registry of weddings, births, and funerals. In one section of the Munsill Papers, he also narrates early "Accidents and Incidents" that glinted as they settled through the slow, clear seasons of a still-unstoried town. This is the most eloquent chapter of his chronicle, and the one that I've searched most attentively in trying to read the character of my home.

The first "Incident" gives the somnolent pages of description a rough shake, making them tick like a clock, or like a heart.

Amze Higby a child between four and five years old son of Nehemiah Higby was killed by the fall of a tree cut by his father on the farm where Samuel Stewart and Eden Johnson first located and where William Dunshee now lives in the following manner, to wit,
    The father Nehemiah Higby was chopping down trees for the purpos of clearing the land and the little sprightly boy was sent by his mother to call his father to dinner and when within a short distance of his father who was then chopping down a tree, with all the animation natural to a child of that age, called out to his father, dinner is on the table, and at that instant when first the father heard the voice of his little son, he discovered that the tree had commenced falling, and that to, in the direction of his beloved son who by the fall of that tree was instantly killed and this was the first death in Bristol.

This first death, like the expulsion of a long-held breath, was the beginning of the town's real history. The name Higby appears nowhere else in the tables of offices held, farms bought and sold. But when the child went down beneath the tree, a vital issue was decided. That settled things. For me, too, as with the old shepherd's loss of his son in the poem "Michael," this loss was an opening. I could enter sympathetically into the history of Bristol, grieving as a parent for the parents of Amze Higby, dead so young. The cycles of geology and of forest succession were humanized by personal cataclysm, brought into the scale of my human heart.
    One other section in the "Accidents and Incidents" of Munsill's history rises to the intensity of Amze Higby's death, and again the central figure is a child.

Orcemus Shumway, about three years old, in the month of June 1806 wandered a way from home following the main travelled road, as is supposed, West from Bristol village to near the top of the hill, called Stoney Hill, and there taking a Woods road leading north into the Woods, and night coming on and dark the Child was unable to find its way home and remained in the Woods alone. Through the night although his anxious parents made diligent search to find him, but without success. Early the next morning notice was given that a Child was lost in the Woods.

This notice was sufficient to call out the inhabitants of Bristol old and young as well as some of the neighboring towns, and who immediately organized in to Companies and formed a line and commenced a march through the Woods, keeping at a proper distance from each other and making a thorough search which continued until about two o-clock in the after noon without making any discoveries; and the Search for a short time suspended, and all returned to the Village.

The Parents of the Child were almost frantic. The question was asked by many what can be done and the response from the many were Search until the Child is found. This seemed to be the unanimous expression, and they again formed in to Companies and formed a line, and by this time assistance had arrived from the neighboring towns and so increased their numbers as to enable them to form a verry extended line, which they did, and then commenced again to search the Woods where they had not before been, and after a diligent Search of about three hours the Child was found setting down by a large pine tree, some what frightened by the sight of so many strangers.

The Child was unhurt when found having followed the Woods road to the terminous and not able to find its way back being in a dense forrest and the Child to young to Exercise any judgement on the occasion. The Child was found a North Westerly direction from the Village.

When the fact was announced that the Child was found and unhurt, the declaration was reasserted with an earnestness that rent the air, and rolled back a rejoining echo, from the mountain, the Lost Child is found.

The writer was himself present on the occasion, and well remembers the good feeling manifested and smiling countenances of all who participated in the Search.

When I first came upon these two "Incidents" in Munsill, I immediately read them aloud as a pair to several friends. I wanted to share the satisfaction of the second Child's recovery, its effect enhanced by the earlier story's shocking loss. It reminded me of the story about when the mail-packet from England sailed into New York Harbor with the final installment of Dickens's *Old Curiosity Shop*. The crowd on the wharf, totally absorbed in the fate of Little Nell, called over the water to the Captain, "Is she dead?" When he shouted back "Dead," the crowd burst into tears. This time, though, the people of Bristol heard "The Lost Child is found," and couldn't stop grinning as they trudged back down to the village. This time the tree stood rooted in its place, sheltering the frightened Child until help came and carried him safely home.

Last week, on October 4th, our fourteen-year-old son Matthew did not come home for dinner at six o'clock. He'd told us that right after school was out he and his friend Benj Hanf were going up on the mountain to put some final touches on a "paleolithic shelter" they were building for their Global Studies class. They were doing a unit on human migrations and cultures in the first part of our present interglacial period, and the chance to fashion spears and other implements had engaged Matthew more than any other aspect of the new high school year. The two boys had built one shelter in a boulder-lea not far above Benj's house, but then forged farther up the broken slope. They'd found a steep overhanging cliff, above a ledge accessible only by a sketchy trail—the perfect hideout for two paleolithic teenagers. With wood and stones they walled in an enclosure against the cliff-face. With clay and chalk and charcoal they decorated the interior of their shelter with images inspired by the mystic hunters of Lascaux. Their original plan had been to bring the class up for a visit when it was completed, but as they switched to a more distant, more precarious site, they decided instead that they'd photograph the final project for a report. A camera and a box of chalk went up with them on this afternoon.

Seven o'clock came, and darkness, with no sign of Matthew. Benj's mother consulted on the telephone with Rita and me, uncertain what to do. Then, at 7:40, I drove to their house, taking a flashlight by which to hike up into the mountains after the boys. Benj's dad Bill was waiting for me by the road with his own flashlight, and together we started toward the rocky knob where he thought they might have gone.

The moon was long past full, and the night so overcast that except for the rippling pools of light around our flashlights total darkness prevailed amid the trees. I'd never hiked this approach to the ridge before, and could only follow Bill's lead. He paused often, looking for the remnant of a logging road that might lead us to the top. I had brought our retriever Maple, thinking she might scent the boys. She dashed around us, whirling up drifted maple leaves in the gusts of her excitement. The three of us ascended in a series of switchbacks until we reached a bouldery boil of land between two north-south ledges. Caves and cliffs were everywhere, still dripping from the afternoon's rain. Our flashlights swept into beautiful, fern-thick grottoes and, finding no lost boys, swung onward, leaving them to darkness.

Once we had made it to the broken height we started to call out for our sons as loudly as we could. "BENJ!" Bill would shout with his booming voice, a percussive call that bounced back to us from unseen cliffs. I sang out "Maaa-theww!" in my tenor, but the cadence always floated off unanswered through the lacy hemlock tops.

Maple was such a panting, scrabbling noisemaker that it was hard at first to tell if there *was* any answer to our shouts. But as the minutes passed she began to stand absolutely still whenever either of us called, and to peer up into our faces as we held our breath, waiting with us for our sons' response.

Only at this point did I remember the stories of the two boys in Munsill's manuscript. In all my days of hiking and writing in the mountains, I had counted on recovering my bearings whenever I got lost. The wilderness all around our home had recovered from the ravaged, muddy slopes of the last century, and I held a familial faith in these providential woods. But what if, after all, Bill and I were hiking up into the *first* of Munsill's two stories, and my lost son were never found? More than once the two of us slid toward a cliff's edge with the collapse of an eroded slope. I began to picture a young body lying beneath a dark overhang, white face suddenly glowing in the flashlight's beam. I seemed to see myself from a great elevation, as well. My father had died seven weeks ago. Since then, my mother had fallen twice within her first day home from surgery. Now this? Dread fell with a rush like the sudden dropping of the temperature.

Bill and I had been climbing and calling, calling for hours, when we finally decided to head back down. Our consoling theory was that it was unlikely *both* boys would have been injured, and that if there had been some accident the uninjured boy would certainly have heard us by now and answered. Failing to receive any response, we therefore figured that either they'd made it safely down on their own or they'd wandered down the *eastern* flank of the mountain. If they weren't waiting at the bottom we'd call the police and fire departments and set up a search-and-rescue team. But in fact we heard a car on the road below, honking rhythmically to summon us home, when we were about halfway back to our starting point.

Benj's high-school-senior brother Brian and his friend Corey had found Matthew and Benj far to the north of where Bill and I were searching. When darkness fell, the two younger boys couldn't make their way out of their paleolithic world to the road and home. So they lit a fire, drew their light jackets around themselves, and settled into their shelter God-knew-where in the woods. Brian tracked them to their firelit lair, then mocked them safely home. Smoky, pale, and uncommunicative, two fourteen-year-olds waited for Bill and me in the headlights of the idling car.

After a microwaved helping of casserole, a glass of cider, and a shower, Matthew hit the sack, and so did Rita and I. I lay close to her side, trying to escape the chill as if sheltering by a fire-warmed over-hang in the darkness of the mountain. But sleep did not come for a long time. I could still feel invisible rocks sliding beneath my boots as I walked down the slope defeated. My flashlight had given out on the return hike, so I'd had to follow closely behind Bill, trying to imitate him when he lifted one foot especially high or stepped to the side to avoid an obstacle. Struggling so hard to concentrate while going blind, I found that the trickling of unseen streams and the earthy smell of wet moss were magnified. And now, in the familiar darkness of our bedroom, I was filled with confused sensations, like a mountain brimming with recollection of the rain.

When an experience takes root in our lives it often grows up into a story. Just as I had wanted earlier to share the two tales from Munsill's history of Bristol, I now found myself telling people about the night of searching for Matthew and his friend by flashlight. The voice in my own ears when I told of this experience was a wry one—just another ridiculous incident in which we had managed to get in-volved. But a few days afterwards I was relating the search to a small group which included a man I'd never met before, and he heard something different in my voice. To judge by his response, he felt real fear within the humor of my story, and not just for the dangers of treacherous terrain after dark. More than I was conscious of my-self, he focused on the struggle of parenting an adolescent whose inner life remained beyond the flickering beam of my flashlight and whose immediate future was still not so clear to me. This man's response was to put a poem by Wendell Berry into my mailbox the next morning. "The Way of Pain" begins,

> For parents, the only way
> is hard. We who give life
> give pain. There is no help.
> Yet we who give pain
> give love; by pain we learn
> the extremity of love.

The gift of this poem from a man I barely knew staggered me. Like Rabbi Reichert's command at that dinner so many years ago, it vaulted over the restraints of courtesy to touch the heart. The unknown, unseen listener was right. The point of my story, I realized now, was parenting and pain. I understood, too, that "a sense of place" would remain a vague concept if founded only in my researches into the natural and human history of Bristol, and in my readings of Frost and Wordsworth. The galvanizing stories of place are finally those we suffer for ourselves.

In Leslie Silko's essay about stories and the Pueblo sense of place, she illustrates her points by telling two stories about the landscape around her home. One is an ancient mythic tale that ties the origin of a gigantic sandstone boulder to the Twin Hero Brothers' rescue of Yellow Woman from the giant Estrucuyo. But the other recounts an event that happened to Silko's own ancestors. "A high dark mesa rises dramatically from a grassy plain fifteen miles southeast of Laguna, in an area known as Swanee," this tale begins. Silko tells that her kinsmen were insufficiently wary while herding sheep near that mesa and thus allowed Apache raiders to surprise them from the other side, steal their sheep, and take their lives. To this day, her people never look at that landform without remembering the story of her careless relatives' murder, never tell the story without seeing that black mesa in their minds' eye.

Our Vermont landscape, like Silko's in New Mexico, begins to contain familial tales of loss. When a wilderness excursion was a self-contained idyll, a several-weeks' vacation from the pressures of job or school, the mountains remained serenely apart—a refreshing world elsewhere. But now that my hikes thread around and around the densely forested ridges of a plateau where our children are growing up, a new intensity and complexity has come into nature. I have an adolescent son I'm deeply worried about; I still feel as if I'm looking for him day and night in rocky terrain, with a failing flashlight; I hike the woods remembering other hikes, other days, and sometimes feeling cut off from my father and my son alike. But these gaps and fears also open a space for the local wilderness to rush into my daily life. Our family's years together here become more vivid because gathered into the mysterious circulation of the rocks and trees.

In the second and third stanzas of Berry's poem, the speaker reads in his Bible about sons and sacrifice—about Abraham and Isaac, and Christ crucified. In the fourth and final stanza he takes those stories into his dreaming heart.

> And then I slept, and dreamed
> the life of my only son
> was required of me, and I
> must bring him to the edge
> of pain, not knowing why.
> I woke, and yet that pain
> was true. It brought his life
> to the full in me. I bore him
> suffering, with love like the sun,
> too bright, unsparing, whole.

Abraham and Isaac, Michael and Luke. Tales of sacrifice cement our covenant with God and with the human community. But the covenant with land too calls for sacrifice, and may involve a loss. The ruined farmstead of "Directive" becomes a more concrete and immediate loss for me as I understand that my family too could lose our lives among these hills, will certainly lose them if we stay here through the seasons that call us home.

Bristol Cliffs

And there's a story in a book about it:
Besides the wear of iron wagon wheels
The ledges show lines ruled southeast-northwest,
The chisel work of an enormous Glacier
That braced his feet against the Arctic Pole.
You must not mind a certain coolness from him
Still said to haunt this side of Panther Mountain.

All along the Green Mountains' western edge are rocky ledges and great exposed knees of stone. But the talus slope at Bristol Cliffs is the flintiest jumble of them all. Vermont's largest expanse of talus, it forms a ragged rectangle of pale gray Cheshire quartzite visible from many miles to the west, constantly renewed as more huge blocks of stone tumble down the over-steepened cliff and jolt up the unlichened bellies of the resting stones to take the sun. At the bottom (west), where the slope finally flattens out, veteran spruces lean their backs against the last slow nudges at the tapering edge of gravity. At the southern margin of the talus, sumacs perch among boulders that have bounced and scattered outward from the main flow. But no trees can withstand the perpetual violence of the talus field itself. Out in the bumptious middle, there's an occasional woody tendril of the native grape, playing the conciliator with an arm across two vast clinched backs but a queasy feeling that this companionable repose will not last long. Under the protection of a few especially mammoth, stable rocks, clumps of herb robert, our local wild geranium, flaunt the lacy greenness of their foliage amid the gray for whatever seasons they are given. Hiking gingerly across the talus, I smell these herb-robert gardens before I see them. They send up aromatic gusts that remind me of the Southwest, and of the pungency of creosote hanging in discrete pockets above the sand.

Grainy facets of quartzite glint in the westering sun. Like the afternoon edition of a paper, these rocks contain the whole, belated story. Of how the minerals of this windy Vermont ridge once formed in an opening of the ocean's crust, compounding as thousands of feet of sediment settled down upon them through the quietness. Of how the European and North American plates collided, wrenched apart, collided again, rearing the parallel ridges of the Green Mountains and the Adirondacks like two long waves, rocks spilling from their crests like foam. Just 12,000 years ago the Wisconsin Glacier melted back toward Canada in its latest strategic retreat, having rounded these summits, scraped away the soil, plucked away whole gaps, scoured out valleys, and mapped where rivers would run, where trees would grow, where human settlements would appear like clusters of herb robert amid the rocks' slow flow.

> And there's a story in a book about it:
> Besides the wear of iron wagon wheels
> The ledges show lines ruled southeast-northwest,
> The chisel work of an enormous Glacier
> That braced his feet against the Arctic Pole.

Following Frost up into the heights, I gain a new sense of what "a story in a book" might mean. The colon at that first line's end invites a connection between the book and the geological processes inscribed on the exposed ledge. This is no "book of nature" in the idealized sense of Duke Senior's "sermons in stones and books in running brooks" in *As You Like It*. It's a messy page, with one sen-

tence scrawled over another. There are the ruts of the early settlers, bringing their wagons in and then, just a few decades later, rolling out of these inhospitable heights again. But besides them, and *beside* them, are grooves left by the glaciers' own southward slide. The stories, like the lines, are parallel. This afternoon, as I clamber up the talus slope on hands and knees, I reverse the rocks' long downward rumble. But as evening approaches, I'll lapse back into the main flow. Gravity will instruct me, as it did the farmers and the ice, on the way to go.

Frost too helps me to grasp what the ledges "show." From his poem's first line he has echoed Eliot's *Waste Land,* attempting to find the pattern that connects within an overwhelming world of fragments. Toward the beginning of "The Burial of the Dead," Eliot writes:

> What are the roots that clutch, what branches grow
> Out of this stony rubbish? son of man,
> You cannot say, or guess, for you know only
> A heap of broken images, where the sun beats,
> And the dead tree gives no shelter, the cricket no relief,
> And the dry stone no sound of water. Only
> There is shadow under this red rock . . .

These lines might describe a traverse of the talus slope as well as a search for respite from the "rubbish" of "all this now too much for us." Frost and Eliot are alike in searching for meaning amid the wilderness of forms, and in eventually connecting their quests explicitly with the Grail and the sacramental narrative of Western spirituality. The difference is that Frost really is interested in the rocks themselves. There is no "rubbish" here for him. In the palimpsest of his Vermont ledges, ordinary people find a grandeur and dignity eluding the denizens of Eliot's London—in part because their path ran beside the glacier's. Frost reads the ledge like an ancient, crumbling *ledger.* The deepest, and deepening, meaning of this landscape is geological and inclusive.

There is a providence in repetition. Just as this region of Vermont is now covered with its third forest since the withdrawal of the Wisconsin Glacier, so too the Green Mountains represent the third distinct version of the Appalachian chain to stretch the length of Vermont. Nine hundred million years ago the North American and African plates collided, thrusting up the proto-Appalachians. In the fullness of time, the plates once more began moving apart and ocean rose up over what had been high ground. The early mountains gradually eroded onto that broad, shallow ocean shelf. But when the plates moved together again in that great joining of continents that geologists call Pangaea, the mineral sediments of North America and those of Africa-Europe crowded each other upward in a process of orogeny, or mountain building, that raised a much loftier Appalachian chain than before. This process lasted from about 500 million years ago to 200 million years ago. As the plates withdrew again, into the present configuration of our continents, the Appalachians once again began a process of erosion.

I began to see how these particular ledges, this particular talus slope, arose from my hikes around Bristol Cliffs with the geologist Lucy Harding, from reading a site-evaluation written by Jeffrey Severson of the University of Vermont's Field Naturalist Program, and from interviewing Ray Coish, another geologist and a colleague at Middlebury. They helped me feel the time, and see the tides, that left this wrack of mountains on the present's shore.

The finely grained quartzite glinting around me now in the talus and ledges of Bristol Cliffs began as Cheshire Formation sands deposited on the ocean shelf 600 million years ago, before the collision of plates that raised the second, higher Appalachians. About 445 million years ago, under the pressure of reconverging plates, these sands were metamorphosed into quartzite and arenite as they were lifted up into a mountain that also combined material from the opposing ocean shelves. This geological event, which lasted until approximately 200 million years ago, spanned the Cambrian, Ordovician, Silurian, and Devonian epochs. Its two main phases were the Taconic Orogeny and the Acadian Orogeny. During the Acadian Orogeny, another stage of carbonate sediments, or "platform units," was raised to overlie the Cheshire Formation in the "stratigraphic column." This is the Dunham Formation, or Dunham dolomite.

Severson describes the remaining ridge of Cheshire quartzites at Bristol Cliffs as the "physiographic boundary between mountain and valley."

Almost the entire 150 kilometer-long western scarp of Vermont's Green Mountains south of [Bristol Cliffs] is formed by the Cheshire Formation. This bedrock control of steep western slopes directly influences the character of regional drainage patterns, and was therefore a key influence on regional settlement patterns, making the Cheshire important culturally as well as geologically. Although the Champlain Valley just to the west of the proposed landmark served as a corridor for human settlement, the rugged cliffs and talus on the mountainside remained essentially wild.

Geology is the epic of this place, of any place. The challenge is to see something so *big,* to focus on a reality so enveloping. As I gaze at the boulders' delicate striations in the warm light of this afternoon, I can picture the process of submarine extrusion, cooling, and compression that gave this quartzite form. For just a moment I can glimpse, up close, what hundreds of millions of years look like. At most other times, though, my best course is to stand back and look for waves. In one geology textbook, I saw a diagram of how anticlines and synclines are related. Anticlines are convex folds on the surface of the earth, with older layers of bedrock breaking through the stretched, attenuated, rising bend. Synclines are concave—troughs in which the older rocks are thrust downward while the newer ones squeeze together thickly near the surface and also catch the newer sediments washed down from the heights. When the sun rose this morning, shadows from Bristol's Hogback Anticline spread out over the Middlebury Synclinorium—as the past always hangs mysteriously over each new present. The quartzite boulders below me now slide like a drift of brown leaves down the steep slope of November. In the next hour, though, as the sun sinks toward the blue transparency of the Adirondack high peaks, brilliant colors will flow back up these boulders toward the ledge like a returning tide.

The Hogback Anticline, which includes both South Mountain and North Mountain, marks where a section of the Cheshire bedrock shifted westward along a thrust fault. But the movement proceeded at different rates along the length of the ridge, causing a break in the anticline and a differentiation between the two mountains. This is what geologists call an "east-west trending strike-slip fault." It is also the decisive geological feature for the town of Bristol. Bristol Cliffs to the south and Deer Leap to the north soar above a notch through which runs the New Haven River, whose potential for mills was one of the first attractions of this site to settlers after the French and Indian War.

In addition to registering the movement of earth's continental plates, these mountains also record a process of glaciation that began about two million years ago. There seem to have been four waves of ice so far, with the most recent glacier melting something like 12,000 years ago. Looking back 20,000 years, when the glaciation here was at its maximum, we find ice approximately one and a half kilometers thick covering this part of Vermont. When it encroached it ground the soil away, assuring that farmers who moved in after the glacier had disappeared would not long make a go of it in these heights. At Bristol Cliffs, it also sheared off the softer layers of rock called Dunham dolomite, exposing outcroppings of durable bedrock from the Cheshire Formation. What remained was Vermont's rocky spine, and when the thawing glacier left an ice dam to the north, this ridge also became the shore for a series of vast inland seas. Lake Vermont lapped against the palisades of Bristol, succeeded by the Champlain Sea when salt water poured into Vermont through the St. Lawrence River Valley, then by another freshwater Lake Vermont, then by a second Champlain Sea. These episodes left many legacies in our landscape of today—not just the skeleton discovered at a Charlotte railroad-cut in 1849, from a whale that had swum in one of the Champlain Seas, but also the gravel and sand pits that line the edge of Bristol's plateau. Westward from Bristol all the way to the present-day Lake Champlain, we now have rich clays from the sedimentation of those ancient bodies of water. The clays of Middlebury, Addison, Shoreham, and Vergennes support prosperous dairy farms, by producing rich crops of feed-corn and hay. Our land up here in Bristol is the gristle at the edge of Addison County's prime agricultural cut.

Thus, when Frost writes of parallel grooves in the capping ledges of the Green Mountains, he's simultaneously pointing to the history of settlement and abandonment and to the geological background that assured that human cycle in advance. John Muir has written, in *The Mountains of California,* of predestination in the formation of Sierra landscapes:

> . . . for the physical structure of the rocks on which the features of the scenery depend was acquired while they lay at least a mile deep below the pre-glacial surface. And it was while these features were taking form in the depths of the range, the particles of the rocks marching to the same music assembled to bring them to the light. Then, after their grand task was done, these bands of snow-flowers, these mighty glaciers, were melted and removed as if of no more importance than dew destined to last but an hour.

In the same vein, Frost would see Vermont's hill-farmers, and the forests that succeeded them, as predestined by the far earlier compounding of those "particles of the rocks."

Something else is going on in these lines from "Directive," as well. Glacier and Arctic Pole are capitalized and, implicitly, personified. They continue the image of giants in the earth introduced by the "great monolithic knees" of line 11. For a reader, books always contribute to a personal map, orienting and coloring our excursions through the outer world. Sometimes the tales of fantasy or whimsy we read to our children have a special adventurous resonance. I do not take up my hiking stick and follow a trail through the woods without remembering the quests of Frodo and his Fellowship of the Ring. When I'm messing about on Lake Champlain in a canoe, Mole and Ratty from *The Wind in the Willows* always come to mind. And on a hike like today's, when I peer closely, if only half comprehendingly, at the glacier's "chisel work" I recall Jill, Eustace, and Puddleglum's journey to the land of the giants in *The Silver Chair,* from C. S. Lewis's *Chronicles of Narnia.* As those three trekked across a frozen plain they fell into a series of trenches that impeded their progress. Only when they looked down on that day's hard going from a castle that was *not* where they were supposed to end up, did they see that those deep cuts in the rock were actually giant letters spelling out UNDER ME. All along, the ledge of stone was presenting them with their directive. But only time and distance, and getting lost, let them discern the message.

From the monolithic knees to the gigantic chisel work, Frost's poem has continued to complicate its tone—in a way that is both playful and serious. The picture of the Glacier bending over the rock with his chisel, feet braced against a supporting pole like a Vermont farmer leaning against a stanchion as he takes his awl to a piece of harness, is a sort of cartoon. But it is a cartoon by Blake—a dramatic representation of the processes through which our world was formed, and of *design* within the physical creation. It accords, too, with the poet's wish to present the landscape as a ghost story, to haunt it and us in order to intensify our awareness of the local and the present. The strange voice, at once taunting and amiable, that enters "Directive" reflects a barely suppressed eagerness to see what the disoriented and discomfited reader will make of all *this* now.

❧ Amid Bristol Cliffs' remarkable display of geological energy, one of the very strangest stories of our mountain has been played out. With natural landscapes, as with people, it may be that fantasies are the wild stories with which we try to get our bearings before gaining the true stories of relationship. But there can also be a wonderful energy to the fantastic, launching us toward more valid connections with a velocity that might otherwise be hard to attain. I find in the tales of Bristol's "money-diggings" the seed for what Barry Lopez would call an "authentic" story. In his essay "Landscape and Narrative," Lopez writes that such a story has "the power to reorder a state of psychological confusion through contact with the pervasive truth of those relationships we call 'the land.'" People, like other animals, may plant seeds inadvertently while going about our business. But there is a providence that governs when such accidents take root.

The legend of buried treasure near the talus slope of Bristol Cliffs goes back just about as far as the history of the town. In 1801, as the community was getting established, with the conclusion of the French and Indian raids and the planting of the first few farmsteads, some boys spotted a grizzled old man digging just to the south of the talus slope. He had no connection they knew of with the other settlers' families that had arrived from Connecticut and New York State in recent years. And when they went over to talk he growled them away and menaced them with his shovel. The boys' fathers were the next party to visit him, and the implied demand within their own words of welcome and inquiry must have been clear enough. He told them his whole story—or at least *a* story. His name was DeGrau, he said, and he was a Spaniard. Long before the Revolution, he had lived for months near this spot with his father and a couple of other adventurers. They had been wandering through the northern Appalachians with their picks and shovels hunting for precious metals, and had struck a seam of silver here. The ore was rich, and they extracted enough to melt down many ingots, living in a cave in this spot far both from settlements and from the military engagements to the west. When they completed the take, however, the French and Indian War was at a high boil, and they had also run through their supplies. So they cached the treasure in a smaller cave, blocked the mouth with stones, plastered it over with mud, and even transplanted moss over the mud to make it look as much as possible like an undisturbed site. When they had returned home and resupplied, and when the local skirmishes had died down, they would return to claim their wealth.

The only one who ever made it back across the ocean and up the Green Mountains' western slope was this old man, DeGrau, hunting for the buried silver of his boyhood. He remembered exactly where the treasure cave had been, he said. But in the intervening decades the talus-skirt had slumped down over it, burying the ledge where they had worked. He pried away among the obstructing boulders, while farmers from the nearby fields dropped by between chores to watch and chat, if not with him then with each other. Within the year DeGrau gave up for good and left, never to return. But the newly minted Vermonters who were so briefly his neighbors kept alive the story about that strange old man whose accent was like none other they'd ever heard, whose fantastic story had gained credibility by having to be prised out of him, and who had kept his smoldering gaze on the ground as his weak old muscles leaned into that waterfall of stone.

In 1888 and 1889 the *Bristol Herald* ran a series of articles by Franklin S. Harvey that picked up the story of "the money diggings" at Bristol Cliffs. Harvey, a native of Bristol and an amateur historian, related how the next, more vivid, chapter of the search for treasure opened.

It may well be supposed that the circumstances awakened much curiosity, and there was much looking and prying around among the rocks. Some time afterward, before the excitement died away, a singular-looking vessel was found under a rock near by. It showed marks of age and had apparently lain there quite a long time. It held about a quart, and no one could tell what it was made of. Its shape differed from anything in domestic use. The father of the writer remembered it well. His impressions regarding it were that it must have been something left by the Indians. It was in the neighborhood a long time, but I am unable to say what became of it.

Whatever it was, it added fuel to the fire. Some claimed it was a crucible, left there by the Spaniards, and from that time forward, the spirit of money-digging ran riot on this wild earth.

Farmers from the district began to investigate their own little claims around the slope, some of them digging energetically there over a period of several years. But the most dramatic development came in 1840, when Uncle Sim showed up. Simeon Coreser, a native of Canada, arrived with six companions "from up near Magog Lake." It wasn't clear just how they'd heard about the diggings, but they arrived with a plan as elaborate and systematic as that of any colonial enterprise. Their stock-option, open to everyone, was that one dollar in food or provisions would entitle an investor to a return of one hundred dollars from the unearthed treasure. Coreser seems to have hurt his back early on in this expedition, so that he couldn't participate in the actual digging itself. But with his massive physique and high spirits, and dressed in "leather breeches and an old sealskin cap," he remained the party's leader. "His business was to disburse the funds and direct operations in general, gain converts to the cause, and so get pecuniary assistance; also to go and see fortune tellers ('conjurers,' he called them), and get directions where to dig."

Uncle Sim seems to have found plenty of conjurers around Addison County in those days, Yankees and French Canadians alike. They told him where the cave was and how much the silver in it was worth (just over three million dollars). They also described what Harvey called the cave's "supernatural sentinels," the spirits who'd been left behind to guard the treasure when the Spaniards abandoned it:

> A dog was whacked on the head and thrown in there. His blood was burned on a rock by moonlight, and the ashes sprinkled over the treasure. He was a dreadful dog; and from that day down, with untiring feet, he dashed around that cave, howling and snuffing at every crack, and ready to tear in pieces all who entered. He was not alone. A boy, with a frightful gash across his throat, paced round and round the glittering pile with a red-hot iron upraised to smite with a vengeful force the sacrilegious hand that dared to touch a single bar of the guarded pile.

Only Simeon Coreser, by uttering certain words the conjurers had imparted to him, could exorcise the spirits. When the cave was found, but before it was actually opened, he must be brought to break the spell, release the tormented guardian spirits, and begin counting out the shares.

➤➤ When I hiked up with Ted Lylis a week and a half ago for my first look at the money-diggings, he took me through the Bristol Subway. Numerous gigantic slabs of ledge have tumbled out into the woods at this point, a few hundred yards south of the main talus slope. They lean up against each other in jagged polygons like the shards of ice that tilt against the shore when a lake breaks up in spring. Beneath these canted walls and roofs of stone run the warren and chambers of the Subway. As we wound our way upslope through the main passageways, we could see sky break through the overcast of rock at certain points, and we could hear the soft rush of springs welling out from the mountain's roots and cooling the air of a warm fall day. We emerged beside several lofty, south-facing

chambers where Coreser's miners lived. No signs of habitation remain in these mossy grottoes except where, on the ceiling of the
largest hall, a blackened circle tells of fires burned through long winter nights while men huddled in their bedrolls between the flames
and the cave's reflecting back-wall.

Only one shaft of the four main excavations remains open, and it
is not the largest one. Still, this hand-dug opening of eight feet by
ten descends for more than forty feet at a 45-degree angle. The labor
that must have been involved in digging out so much bedrock with
pick and shovel staggered me. Ted told me that, when he moved to
his nearby house in the 1970s, an old-timer informed him that beyond the shaft itself there used to be a cavern big enough to stand
up in and wide enough to stage a dance. With some friends and a
cold keg lowered into the earth, Ted removed the rubble that had
blocked the shaft and confirmed that this underground hall did ex-
ist. Three more shafts issued forth from it, following essentially level
courses to north and south, as well as straight eastward toward the
mountain's heart. On the chamber's walls he found the marks where
miners had punched their chisels' x-cut ends into the stone to make
a purchase for their picks.

The mouth of the shaft was furred with moss and overhung with
common polypody. With Christmas fern, this is one of our two
main evergreen ferns, growing so thickly on shady forest boulders
that its rippling texture earned the common name of rock
tripe—*tripe de roches*—from French Canadians in this part of the
world. As I peered down the dark descent, the shaft curved mysteriously to the north and out of sight.

The ferocious energy of these treasure hunters threw up huge
heaps of tailings all around the shaft. They're now covered with
moss and ferns and subsiding into the churning slump of these steep
woods. But when latter-day treasure hunters arrive, they often fix on
one of these piles as the "oven-shaped opening" of DeGrau's treas-
ure-cave, according to Ted, and once more move around rocks that

have already been shifted by their predecessors. Just down the hill from the remaining open shaft is a depression that was once the opening of the largest excavation—which plummeted almost one hundred feet straight down. The treasure hunters stopped digging here when they struck a pocket of underground gas and the canary that they lowered with them died. Then they converted that whole shaft into a dump for tailings from the subterranean chamber just next door.

The local name that has stuck for this jumble of greed and energy is Hell's Half Acre. The area of the diggings is actually many times bigger than a half acre, but the alliteration offers a joking commentary on the damned strange story of this race for wealth. It's interesting that the heights above the diggings, though not showing any of the miners' handiwork, nonetheless have similarly hellish names. The dramatic, isolated jut of rock at the very top of Bristol Cliffs is called the Devil's Pulpit, while the deeply incised notch down which loggers shot their logs in winter when the run was iced and slick is still known as the Devil's Cart Road. Just as the grooves in the ledge registered the parallel migrations of settlers and glaciers, so too the frenzy of the miners and the broken heights both seemed to violate the normal decorums of a Vermont landscape. The talus slope, too, received a name that would have struck the farmers as diabolical. It was called Rattlesnake Den, and the townsfolk who came up to inspect the mines also partook in Sunday afternoon rattlesnake hunts. The snakes would already have been long gone from this slope when Harvey wrote his *Bristol Herald* articles at the end of the last century, but they still played an important part in his evocation of Devil's Pulpit, as viewed from below in Hell's Half Acre:

> It is nearly square in form and its angles are sharply defined—a regular monumental shaft, standing up against the side of the mountain.

Such is the Devil's Pulpit, and as we gaze upward toward it the old tale comes back to our minds, of how, in prehistoric times when griffins walked the earth and troops of gigantic mastodons were wading across Lake Champlain and cooling their sides in its sparkling waters, His Cloven-footed Majesty used to mount up there and preach to the rattlesnakes, taking "pizen" for his text. What a preacher and what a congregation!—just think of them, swarming on the rocks, their heads raised to catch a view of the speaker and their eyes glittering with excitement as some thrilling burst of demoniac oratory attracts their attention!

All that energy, poured out to penetrate beneath the talus and unearth the treasure, was the enactment of a dream. The Spanish silver, and the stock-option company to which it gave rise, was a fantasy—an "illusion" in Freud's sense of something we believe not primarily because of external evidence but because we *need* to believe it. This is more than a derogatory term, however. King Lear always wrings my heart when he begs his daughter, "O reason not the need." Which of us would ever summon up the energy to find our way in life or truly make a home unless impelled by needs which we are far from understanding completely? Geologists today confirm that, though silver was once found in commercial quantities down around Plymouth, Vermont, it would never appear in a geological formation like Bristol Cliffs. Often, in looking back at our forebears in the New World, we glimpse such extravagant, or compulsive, behavior as they try to root unseen wealth out of the earth. But out of mistakes and obsessions may grow familiarity and relationship. Even holes dug down into the exposed bedrock, rifts opened in the fabric of nature, may come to serve a larger purpose. Gaps, in a rocky land, allow for new root-tips to enter the ground and for new shoots to be sheltered. Herb robert flourishes amid the brokenness of the talus slope.

Wordsworth's "Nutting" helps me make sense of the money-diggings. Like so many of his poems, it tells a story. At the beginning, a boy sets out to gather hazelnuts. Costumed for adventure, he makes his way deeper and deeper into the woods until he comes to an absolutely prime hazel-grove, thick with nuts and with no sign of other people having been there for years. The boy pauses in the quiet grove to hear

> the murmur and the murmuring sound,
> In that sweet mood when pleasure loves to pay
> Tribute to ease; and of its joy secure,
> The heart luxuriates with indifferent things,
> Wasting its kindliness on stocks and stones,
> And on the vacant air.

The destructiveness that erupts in the poem right after these lines is forecast by the words "indifferent" and "vacant." The boy is unconnected with the natural scene until, in an impulse that might seem to come from nowhere in the poem, he suddenly begins to rip down hazel limbs. This shocking scene gives way as abruptly to a sense of identification with the violated woods.

> Then up I rose,
> And dragged to earth both branch and bough, with crash
> And merciless ravage: and the shady nook
> Of hazels, and the green and mossy bower,
> Deformed and sullied, patiently gave up
> Their quiet being: and, unless I now
> Confound my present feelings with the past,
> Ere from the mutilated bower I turned
> Exulting, rich beyond the wealth of kings,
> I felt a sense of pain when I beheld
> The silent trees, and saw the intruding sky.—
> Then, dearest Maiden, move along these shades
> In gentleness of heart; with gentle hand
> Touch—for there is a spirit in the woods.

Providence can take the oblivious destructiveness of human beings as its vehicle in the world. On the talus slope beneath Bristol Cliffs, people spent the first century of our town's existence playing with large blocks and digging in the sandbox. The question is, what comes next, as we walk the defaced ledge and listen for the sounds of home.

The following lines in "Directive" both bring the arch personification of geology to its completion and begin the transition to another level of Bristol Cliffs' natural history, the return of wildness after the retreat of the hill-farmers:

> You must not mind a certain coolness from him
> Still said to haunt this side of Panther Mountain.

The glacier lingers in the coolness of an overhanging cliff, just as extinct mountain lions are called to mind by the mountain that still bears their name. Presence within absence is Frost's theme, and my own. Following up on the implied personification of his capitalized terms, the poet now refers to the Glacier directly as "him." Coolness haunts the mountain, representing the temporarily absent Glacier, like the wryness sharpening the air of Frost's poem after we have given ourselves to the forest on his instruction.

Coolness, wryness, and detachment are stereotypical characteristics of the "old Vermonter." Such aloofness registers a proud sense of priority in the landscape—like the coolness of a Glacier who was present at the creation. But what might strike a newcomer to Vermont as mere cantankerousness is eventually revealed, in a surprising number of cases, both to express mischievous humor and to invite a conversation that delves beneath the surface of social niceties. I've learned a little about this surprising combination of coolness and high spirits from two of our neighbors here in Bristol village.

I have a neighbor, just down Pine Street from where it dead-ends into our side lot, who maintains a small-engine repair shop in his garage as a sideline. I've bought several ten- or fifteen-dollar lawn-mowers from Ed over the years, and trundled them back and forth to his shop many a time for resuscitation, sharpening, or, finally, trade-ins. He usually does the necessary repairs while I wait, and we have always enjoyed chatting with each other on such occasions. Still, I turn my mower down his long driveway with a sense of trepidation. There he is at the garage door, pipe clamped between his teeth and staring at me expressionlessly for the rattling eternity of my approach. When I do come up to him, as often as not he turns away to putter with something on his workbench before finally tossing a remark over his shoulder. But these encounters, though they always begin with my feeling a bit chilled, invariably end most cordially. The only real difficulty is politely extricating myself from a conversation Ed seems eager to prolong.

My next-door neighbor Ezra Dike, who died two years ago, had a riding mower that Ed always came over to our side of the road to fix. And I noticed one day that when Ed walked down Ez's driveway he got the same long, blank stare I got on my Pine Street crossings. Ez was the older man, and his was one of the founding families of Bristol. Beyond these forms of priority, he had simply had more practice staring and waiting. At his funeral, we heard the story about Dennis Maloney calling Ezra up in his capacity as a lawyer when he moved to town more than twenty-five years ago, in order to have Ez do the closing on his house. They made an appointment to meet at a certain Main Street address at a certain time, but when Dennis showed up he found that it was the general store. Not realizing that Ez was also the store's proprietor, Dennis sat down on the step to wait for his lawyer. After half an hour, no one had come, and he decided he must have gotten the wrong address. Since he was there anyway, he thought he might as well go into the store and look around. Just on the other side of the plate-glass door, sitting in a chair and looking out at the steps, was Ezra, whose greeting was, "I wondered how long you were going to sit there."

This is not exactly benign, nor what we might think of as good manners, but it is at least *interesting*. It's a challenge to one's composure, like a children's contest to see who can go longer without blinking. In the Vermont woods, too, we are nettled—led on by everything we don't yet see and can't clearly hear. Silence and absence teach us to pay attention. They throw us upon our own resources. Going up the driveway, waiting outside the store, or hiking up into the scrubby woods above Bristol, we intend to transact some business. But we may suddenly realize we're being watched. Such a turning of the tables transforms an ordinary moment into a pulse-raising challenge.

When Frost wrote "Directive" in 1946, the name Panther Mountain would have seemed another kind of relic in the woods, since most larger wildlife except the white-tail deer had long vanished in Vermont. Like the glacier itself, or like the Abenaki people notably not mentioned in this poem, panthers, or catamounts, were conspicuous in their absence. This was the historical moment the poem limns so precisely. Vermont was much more wooded than when Frost had first settled in northern New England almost half a century before, but considerably less so than today. We have to fix him precisely in this time, out of respect for his poem's precision—and as a way to take seriously the links it forges between a specific time and place and the grand themes of recovery and communion.

Just as we read within the context of all the other books we've read, so too the meaning we find in any poem always reflects the specifics of our own time and place. My place, like Frost's, is the western slope of the Green Mountains. But in my time there are far fewer hill-farms than in his and far more wild animals. When our family moved to Addison County twenty-one years ago, the only moose one ever heard of was the occasional dopey and unwell one that straggled down Route 7, followed by a state policeman making sure no one hurt it and a cavalcade of kids on bicycles who were not about to miss a parade led by a police car and a moose. Now we have a healthy and growing population of moose year-round. Hiking down the Long Trail on Mt. Abraham just last fall, I met a man whose forearms were red and scraped from his having just shinnied up a tree to escape a large bull moose's charge. The black bear population is up, too. And for years now, people have been saying that the catamounts, or panthers, have come back. For just as many years the state Fish and Game people have been vigorously denying their existence here. By the end of this past summer, though, even they have admitted there are panthers in Vermont once more, on the basis of some scat found near Woodstock. A DNA analysis of it confirmed both the species and the presence of at least two different individuals. Haunting, then, can be the bridge between what was, amid these mountains, and what may be again. It can remind us of a world beyond lawnmowers and real estate, a possibility for adventures "back out of all this now too much for us."

➤➤➤ Immediately to the south of the money-diggings is a flat tan ledge where the Barker Kiln once stood. The kiln was not a permanent structure of any kind, but simply the site where huge pyramids of logs were carefully stacked up. The art was in establishing an oxygen-poor fire in the interior of the pile and using it to reduce huge quantities of wood to charcoal for the furnaces that smelted iron by the New Haven River. Farmers in Bristol Flats would not have seen an orange conflagration when they looked up to the ledge at night. Rather, there would have been a steady column of smoke, a curtained glow, and occasional bursts of sparks as wood was loaded in or charcoal removed. Yet this was the holocaust that destroyed the second forest of Vermont.

Holocaust originally meant a burnt offering to God, a sacrifice through which not only the animal offered but the ones offering it were made holy. In its evolution throughout the Bible, it became the outward sign of inward purification, as when Abraham showed his faith through willingness to sacrifice his only son to God and *then* the sacrificial ram was found in the thicket. In our own day, the word has become attached to the Nazi Holocaust in which millions of people were murdered. It has thus taken on a radically different meaning—that of an atrocity beyond comprehension. Our reference to holocaust in such a context expresses the dumbfounding of faith in the face of such enormity. In this modern sense, the word is now also increasingly applied to environmental destruction. Edward Hoagland is one writer who has described the loss of wild habitat, the extinction of species, and the rupture of atmospheric and oceanic systems as a holocaust.

As I stand here on the ledge where the Barker Kiln once smoldered, I want to believe in the possibility for a transforming *sacrifice* within the heedless destruction of the woods. The returning wilderness of Vermont provides a unique vantage point here, dramatically different from the West Coast perspective of the environmental movement. In California, where the Sierra Club and the wilderness-ethos were incubated, wildness was seen as a resource that could only be destroyed. Civilization was often presented figuratively as a cancer, creeping outward into the wild places in ways that left them permanently spoiled, with suburbs as the encroaching ganglia and air pollution as the clouded blood. There were compelling reasons for seeing things that way in a landscape where the wilds were so spectacular, the growth of human population so extravagant, and the climate so dry that vegetation took decades to recover along the earthmover's tracks.

Rita watched her girlhood home in the Santa Clara Valley transformed within just a few years from the fruit-basket of America to the suburban sprawl and freeways of Silicon Valley. When she was growing up, an annual highlight of spring was the Blossom Festival. But she's haunted to this day by the image of a cherry orchard near her town being bulldozed in full flower to make way for the latest subdivision. One by one, the white clouds of blossoms, with their pollinating bees, were laid low in the dust. Our own children, by contrast, have grown up on the edge of mountains growing wilder year by year, and have watched the moose return as permanent neighbors within their lifetimes. Last summer for the first time we stood behind our house and heard coyotes singing to the moon up on the nearby ridge. The arrival of their song, like the authentic narratives Barry Lopez describes, bore a power "to nurture and to heal, to repair a spirit in disarray."

Today, I am up above the talus slope of Bristol Cliffs, in a wilderness thickly forested and rich with animal life where few trees stood just a little over a century ago. The people who lived and worked along these heights—like the family whose abandoned farmstead Frost takes us to in "Directive"—are long gone. Vermont thus shows that wilderness can overtake civilization, rather than always working the other way around. It reminds us that nature is not just a congressionally mandated reserve, protected within the green line of its official proclamation boundary. Nature also surrounds and defines our settlements. The model here is less like combat in which only one side can prevail than like a traditional Vermont contradance, an intricate shuttle that weaves individual dancers into a larger, always altering, design. At this stony eruption above the wet fields of Bristol Flats, our town's new citizens dug for buried treasure and sent a forest up in smoke to raise some cash. Now, when those feverish days have given way to mossy shafts sinking far into the rock and a blackened ceiling of stone amid the trees, a residuum of stories lingers on. Reflecting on the rocks, the plants, and the human activities at this talus slope, we can begin to imagine a more inclusive dream of home.

>>> As an amateur naturalist trying to atone for my liberal education, I dutifully carry a little stack of field guides with me on my hikes. Today, my beloved Newcomb's wildflower guide is joined in the rucksack by Peterson's guides to ferns and eastern trees. Here on the western face of Bristol Cliffs, the upward progression of the trees had always bewildered me until recently. Then Alicia Daniel of the Field Naturalist Program at the University of Vermont gave me a copy of Michael Shepherd's master's project. He studied forest development above and below several New England talus slopes, with a special emphasis on Bristol Cliffs. What he discovered was that the species of trees one would expect to find higher up the slope, like red spruce and paper birch, were dominant below the talus, while deciduous species one might have looked for at elevations decidedly below those trees, like red maples, butternut, and hophornbeam, grew at the top. This inversion of the anticipated order reflects the fact that as snow melts on sunny days it runs downslope under the talus and refreezes on the shaded ground below. Sphagnum moss insulates the accumulated ice-pack and reduces the temperature at the bottom by as much as eight degrees Celsius from that prevailing in the deciduous zone above. Surprising and intricate effects like this make the topography of Bristol Cliffs seem somehow thicker than that of other woods I've walked. Overturned expectations often prolong my expeditions here—making some day-hikes, in which I've been dead lost just six miles from my home, seem positively like adventures.

The Green Mountains have already risen and fallen twice along this spine, and here they are again. The glaciers have possessed and abandoned this landscape four times, and we can already feel on the wind their fifth approach. We hike through the thickening woods of Vermont's third-growth forest, watched by returning slit-eyed ghosts just out of sight. We climb the ledges, read the grooves, and scramble back down the talus slope to where the cool breath of the heights flows out into the mountain valleys like a memory and an invitation.

The Plane on South Mountain

NEAR NORTH POND
DECEMBER 29, 1994

> Nor need you mind the serial ordeal
> Of being watched from forty cellar holes
> As if by eye pairs out of forty firkins.

This morning, near the beginning of my hike, I paused at the top of Devil's Pulpit and peered down over the precipice at Bristol Cliffs. To my south tumbled the unruly energy of the talus slope, while just inches away on my other side a sharp-edged notch plunged like a chimney down the wall of solid rock. I was sitting in a miniature meadow—a patch of bleached and rustling grasses separated by a little scarp of quartzite from the upward boil of woods. Whenever I come here at the end of May this sunlit shelf is filled with pink lady's slippers, their stems as thick as those of tulips, their translucent petals swirling with blood-red veins. They are as sensuous as any product of the tropics. High-bush blueberries ripen here in July, holding their sweetness even as they wizen and blacken into September. Now, in late December, the berries are almost all detached from their scratchy twigs, and only ice blooms in this little field. Clear ropes of it are bound across the boulders' seams. White crystals skin the low spots of my smooth gray bench. Earth-tinged trunks of ice descend through the chasm to my right, dripping their yellow roots toward the distant ground.

The tallest trees of Bristol Cliffs grow around this crowning vantage point. They are a grove of red pines, opportunists who wedged in here decades ago when the soil beneath the boulders was laced with charcoal from a forest fire. Such pines relish the alchemy of fire, but cannot tolerate shade. So these lofty trees with their temple-column trunks grow as close to the edge as they can possibly find a footing, then lean westward toward the Adirondacks with their top-heavy boughs open to the full afternoon sun. The bark of red pines seems exotic against the more muted tones of beech and maple and the darker trunks of other evergreens. Separate medallions of light gray and soft orangy pink are loosely affixed to the smoother under-bark. I can look past these luminous pines to the Adirondacks— Marcy, Giant, Whiteface, Upper and Lower Wolfjaws. They face the Green Mountains, bounding the Champlain Bioregion on the west as our ridge does on the east. Below, and almost out of sight, shines a ribbon of Lake Champlain itself, broadening as it flows northward until finally dividing, around South Hero and Grand Isle, into a dou-ble-chambered heart.

As I stood, then turned to hike farther up the wooded ridge sur-mounting the Cliffs, I entered a dusky world. Within twenty paces, I had no more views in any direction. None of these hemlocks or beech approached the red pines in height. But whereas the pines rose javelin-straight for many feet before their first whorl of branches, these low-boughed, twisted trees seemed to crouch over me as I hiked. They obscured the sky, whispering around my face and arms as I searched for a clear way up the slope. The ground it-self, with its rocks and moss encased in domes of ice, seemed to close in now. Though the slope was still ascending steeply, it offered the perplexity of a gigantic, inclined washboard rather than the invita-tion of a smooth ramp. Treading up and down, up and down, with low walls of littered earth both before and behind me, I consulted my watch, my compass, and the topo map in plodding toward des-tinations I would not catch sight of till I got there. If I did get there. In my study at home, I have an old brown photograph from the first decade of the century, showing this hill devoid of trees and parceled out into squares by stone walls. But I couldn't find any west-east line of stones to set my course by this morning. Rather, there were just occasional little piles of rock blurring into the general sine wave of the rising woods. After this last glimpse of sky along the edge, I had to stumble higher into a haunted and disorienting world.

> Nor need you mind the serial ordeal
> Of being watched from forty cellar holes
> As if by eye pairs out of forty firkins.

By specifying the "serial" nature of his poem's "ordeal," Frost emphasizes *movement,* in space as well as in time, and in body as well as in mind. Up the mountain, deeper into the woods that close around the western jumble of exposed rock—this is where he now asks his reader to walk, and to reflect. The ragged boughs of hemlock close around, as a poem that began in a graveyard turns to haunting, and to animals that may be watching even now. The poem's first allusion to haunting came earlier, in connection with that legacy of coolness "still said" to linger near Panther Mountain. But now the creepy sense of being watched becomes much more pointed and direct. Woods-fear is an experience of disorientation amid the mysteriously knowing woods—that flickering environment of half-heard rustles in the trees. Whatever the associations of his word may have been for Frost, "serial" also suggests "killer" for a reader of today's newspapers. While the final goal of "Directive" may be to root readers more firmly in this region, and to enhance the landscape's human meaning for us, its main effect at this stage of the climb is to unsettle.

As with the poem's earlier glimpses of giant forms within the landscape, though, there is also a certain *playful* effect in these lines. "Eye pairs" is a nice touch, suggesting the disembodied, winking white circles that come alive in the pitch blackness of a cartoon forest or haunted mansion. We know there are watchers there, but won't know who or what they are until the lights go on. But even with this latest "as if," Frost is again strictly accurate in his imagery, never merely fanciful. A landscape where a forest is rerooting itself amid the vestigial clearings of abandoned farms is an environment rich in edges and inhabitants. Where a field-to-woodland ecotone prevails, the population of white-tail deer explodes. Those timid browsers can venture out into the high grass while never being far from the comfort of dark woods.

The wariness of humans coming to such an edge is fully reciprocated by that of the woodland watchers, as in the encounter Frost offers in his poem "Two Look at Two." A deer peers out at the couple who have walked hand in hand up into the gathering darkness of a mountainside:

> A doe from round a spruce stood looking at them
> Across the wall, as near the wall as they.
> She saw them in their field, they her in hers.
> The difficulty of seeing what stood still,
> Like some up-ended boulder split in two,
> Was in her clouded eyes: they saw no fear there.

"Field" is itself a sort of edge—one of those words doing double duty in Frost's poem. The humans and the deer stand on opposite sides of the wall and also have very different kinds of *visual* fields. They watch intently, but only dimly guess what the other might be seeing. Under the cover of grass cropped by those deer lives yet another realm of numerous, if not so often visible, creatures. Around the grass's roots tunnels a society of mice and voles. In the tangles of sumac and blackberry that encroach upon such feral meadows—translating the flat green vector upward into trees—rabbits abound, hopping through the thicket in a sibilant blur. Many little eye pairs to blink out at humans hiking into the unfamiliar shade. Creatures, like us, looking for life more abundant along the edge.

I love the "forty firkins," too—an odd word that flags the poet's wild range of allusions, the ragged, fecund edges flourishing within Frost's verse. Who would have expected to find Ali Baba and his forty

thieves hanging out amid the third-growth forests of Vermont? But this reference is not a specious one, and not even finally such a stretch. In the world of Scheherazade, too, wild transformations propelled the tales. There was big magic in little lamps, and sworded soldiers curled up patiently within the quiet storeroom's jars. The storyteller's flights of fancy harmonize with the specifics of this mountainside, where farms and fields have been transformed back into the dense life of a forest. They also accord with the encompassing swirl of evolution, and the dance of mutually accommodating ecosystems. Steve Young, a paleo-botanist, once spoke to me about the "antic" quality of evolution. The mutations that drive life through its many varying vehicles are akin to the revolutions of an abandoned field. Such processes of emergence make an arresting spectacle, like thirty clowns clambering out of one small car or forty warriors leaping out of jars. The reality of a mountain's life has as much to do with our wildest dreams as with the sober routines of our daily work.

The many cellar holes that appear in Frost's landscape are especially true to the Vermont he knew from the earliest years of the twentieth century up until the publication of "Directive" in 1946. The first great abandonment of hill-farms took place in the mid-nineteenth century. A half century later the untended houses had sagged and collapsed, leaving only the cellar holes. Many of those old cellars in Frost's woods are themselves now caved in or overgrown, but I recently found a perfectly preserved one in the woods about halfway between here and Ripton. It was a skillful farmer who squared these smooth gray walls and trig corners, using only unmortared field stone. I hopped down into the space where this family would have stored its flour, potatoes, salted meats, and other staples through the long Vermont winter. Walled in by ancient craftsmanship, a guest in the home of a family whose name I did not know, I lingered for a few quiet minutes. My back was against a mature red maple, rooted in this cellar but lifting its branches up through what would have been the kitchen, and rearing its crown over what would have been the roof. Sitting there below the ground, I felt, oddly, as if I myself were a watcher from the past—observing the serial tosses of the world of leaves above, rising from the seed pool of earlier lives. Such incongruous moments are this forest's truth. In learning to read Bristol Cliffs, I've searched them out.

➤➤➤ Last August I followed an abandoned logging road up from Rocky Dale, at the northern edge of the Bristol Cliffs Wilderness Area, looking for the hulk of a World War II fighter plane that crashed into South Mountain on October 24, 1945. I had learned about this old catastrophe when my next-door neighbor, Audrey Dike, showed me the clippings about it in her scrapbook. A Curtiss Helldiver with two Navy pilots aboard was returning to its base in Rhode Island after having taken part in a military air show in Burlington. But the clearance was low that afternoon, and the pilots somehow lost track of their altitude. Audrey told me that, when the stocky, single-prop plane sheared through the trees and met the ground, an explosion rattled windows in the village of Bristol.

I wanted to see beech trees reaching through those broken wings, shuffling history back into the forest's fluttering deck. But there was no plane to be found on this summer afternoon, despite the fact that I'd gotten directions from two people in town who had seen it for themselves. One had said to turn straight up the main ridge from the outlet of North Pond, then walk due south for twenty minutes. The other said to strike a line at 220 degrees southwest from the pond; I would find myself climbing up a cut to the mountain's highest bog. There, amid hemlocks and spruce, I would discover the wreck. Neither of these routes worked for me, though. Hardwoods and puckerbrush grew so thickly in that season that it was hard to follow any line, while the corrugated terrain left me uncertain where the actual ridge was.

I soon realized that my directions would never bring me to the plane, so I began simply to crisscross the mountain's eastern face where it went down. Sometimes I would glimpse the bluish needles of a hemlock, spruce, or white pine and stumble toward them, looking down with every second step because of toppled trees and branches littering that wind-torn slope. My heart lifted whenever a patch of sunlight made a granite slab or a beech tree gleam like alloy. But I soon lost hope each time, perceiving that I was not, after all, at the scene of a disaster.

I walked for six hours, up hill and down, looking for the human incident with which to point this narrative of nature. The missing plane was so much in my mind that I registered little of what I actually saw. My hearing was sharpest to the buzz of small craft passing overhead. "They're leading me," I thought—or, more ambivalently, "What if they should crash at the exact spot?"

I never found the plane on that August hike. A broader circle through the woods, and through the seasons, was required before I reached the wreck. And now, on this clear day in late December, our family's retriever Maple and I have set out to approach North Pond from a new angle. It was a bright morning as we left home, holding at around 30 degrees, and the roads in our village were bare. So I wore my running shoes in order to get up to the ridge faster, and to have more time before dark to comb the hummocky slope for the wreckage that had eluded me on the previous attempts.

In running up the old logging road above the Kilbournes' driveway, I observed how just a couple of hundred feet in additional elevation turned the ground white. At the trail's beginning, frost coated the twig-strewn track so heavily that it formed an icy lattice. As I jogged uphill the interstices filled in, smoothing the grid into a blank new page. I slowed to a walk as the snow reached ankle deep. But Maple continued to career over logs, her reddish golden fur looking warm and alive against the frozen world.

The line we followed to the ridge brought us out on the Bristol side of North Pond, so we had to backtrack along an outlet creek that trickled from the stump-surrounded stockade of a beaver dam. The beaver's pond, with its thatchy, conical lodge, extended north-south in a little valley of its own. Maple and I slid along the ice until it led us to North Pond—a perfect oval set among steeply surrounding hills. Blueberry bushes grow thickly along the western slide, their tough leaves leathery and purple at this season.

I clambered up the slope, heading for the "heighth" of land where one North Street neighbor told me the plane would lie. But, as Maple and I climbed up and down during the next two and a half hours, I realized once again how hard it was to tell which portion of that broken and interfolded range was actually the crowning ridge.

Just before giving up once more, so as to make it back down to the car before darkness came on this short December day, I spotted the hub of one of the plane's wheels. It rose against the gray-white background in an arc of patchy blue metal, its curve highlighted by a ring of ice within the hub. I scrambled down into a little swale to take a look at this wreck so little like what I had imagined. In my mind's eye, there had been a largely intact fuselage of silvery aluminum with the wings still attached, though perforated by straight young beeches. What I actually found were hunks of green or blue metal scattered around a circle almost thirty yards in diameter. It looked as if a plane made of ice had struck a rock and shattered.

The biggest remnant was the engine block. Huge, finned cylinders rotated out from the block proper, with a massive shaft showing where the single propeller was attached. In addition to the engine and the single wheel, I found part of the tail assembly, as well as pieces of the wings and belly. Only the wing flaps remained totally undamaged. Curved sheets of metal perforated with circular holes an inch in diameter, they would have slid out to slow the plane when it went into a dive—delivering the thousand-pound bomb carried internally in a Helldiver.

Explosion and decay have obviously been helped out, in the demolition of this plane, by souvenir hunters. No insignia remained, though on one scrap I did see the single tip of a white star, shining from what was formerly the rim of a painted blue circle. The tail itself, the propellers, the windows, the landing gear, the control panel, and the seats have all been carried away. I've heard that two machine guns originally mounted on the wings were skidded down to North Pond and sunk out of harm's way. And I have to admit that I carried one relic away with me, too—a twisted piece of olive-drab aluminum the size of a fallen leaf. It's here beside me as I write, on the table by my computer.

It figures that I found the plane in early winter. The bewildering foliage of those hardwood groves had all rotated underfoot, and much of the brush had been knocked down by the early storms. In his entry for January in *A Sand County Almanac,* Aldo Leopold wrote,

> The months of the year, from January up to June, are a geometric progression in the abundance of distractions. In January one may follow a skunk track, or search for bands on the chickadees, or see what young pines the deer have browsed, or what muskrat houses the mink have dug, with only an occasional and mild digression into other doings. January observation can be almost as simple and peaceful as snow, and almost as continuous as cold. There is time not only to see who has done what, but to speculate why.

Like all people who live in snowy regions, Vermonters are familiar with this process of reduction and focus. The cold months settle into our state as a gradual clarification. Winter holds up objects in high relief—boulders sealed in globes of ice, strawberry-colored blades of grass twisted through the frozen lacework at a pond's edge—for our most careful regard. It invites us to be still and cool, to let one curve, one color truly enter the mind.

Winter is just one of the erasures through which Vermont has come into its own. Leopold had originally planned to call his book *A*

Sauk County Almanac, after the Wisconsin county where he worked at reclaiming a worn-out farm. But "Sand County" is inclusive of a broader locale—any of the districts across the United States where erosion, drought, deforestation, or just plain bad soil uprooted farming communities and replanted the fields with a new growth of trees. Much of northern New England and upstate New York belongs in Sand County, a landscape in which loss and gain are inextricable.

Although Vermont was the fastest-growing state earlier in the century, two of every five Vermonters departed in the period between 1850 and 1900. Economic stagnation prevailed right up until 1946, the year of "Directive"'s publication. During decades in which many parts of the country were ravaged by the earthmovers of prosperity, Vermont grew wilder and greener every year. Still, there was too much suffering in these failed homesteads to allow for easy celebration, and a legacy of poverty lingers around many hilltowns like Bristol. What's more, the pleasant stability of Vermont is being pressed hard today. The telecommunications revolution, with the decentralized way of doing business it makes possible, turns quiet little worlds like this into targets for settlement, and for exploitation more abrupt than anything Vermont saw in its heyday a century and a half ago. Subdivisions often seem to take the names of farms and forests they have replaced. I expect the next one between Bristol and Burlington to be called "Sand County Estates." This winter, as snow briefly muffles the sounds of construction along Routes 7 and 100, offers a chance to retell the story of Vermont, in preparation for the coming season of distraction.

The wilderness areas designated in Vermont during the past twenty years are the climax of a century of enhancement through impoverishment. The Eastern Wilderness Act of 1975 (inspired in part by Vermont's George Aiken) set aside lands that, while not pristine or vast like wilderness in the West and Alaska, still possessed natural qualities worthy of preservation. Bristol Cliffs Wilderness Area was thoroughly cut over in the past century, and it still turns up the stone and metal testaments of previous owners. This is no "virgin wilderness."

Such rugged land along the heights is from one view just a discarded scrap. But a map of the state shows that our six wilderness areas—a total of 59,421 acres distributed along the Green Mountains' north-south axis—are also Vermont's green heart. Bristol Cliffs, Bread Loaf, Big Branch, Peru Peak, Lye Brook, and the George D. Aiken Wilderness (east of Bennington) focus a landscape where nature and culture have circled toward balance in a surprising, retrograde progression. By statute, wilderness areas cannot be logged or built in. No new roads will be added, and existing ones will be allowed to fade away. While politicians propose plans for developing industry and broadening the tax base, these covenanted acres affirm a connection between Vermont's natural beauty and its century outside the mainstream. Equally valuable to me, though, is the fact that the dense forests along these tracts are often fairly new, and that they are in fact littered with reminders of previous chapters in our history. They show that wildness can grow out of, and transform, the clearings of society. We don't always have to travel to Glacier National Monument or the Gates of the Arctic to find wilderness; under certain circumstances, it can come home to where we live.

These are the ironies of wilderness in many parts of the Northeast. This region, which was among the first parts of the country to be heavily settled, is now growing wild. Failing enterprises cleared the ground for a new attempt at balance with the natural environment. And the abundant rainfall here allows the landscape to reassert its own agenda with a quickness unimaginable in states west of the hundredth meridian.

When I finally found the plane on today's hike, I remembered my neighbor's word "heighth," in his description of where to search for the wreck. It reminded me of some lines that come further on in "Directive":

> The height of the adventure is the height
> Of country where two village cultures faded
> Into each other. Both of them are lost.

The wreckage of the Helldiver and the failed homesteads of Vermont show where lives, and whole communities, have been lost. But they also point to places where human vestiges and the region's nonhuman life have begun to fade together, lost in an emerging balance of wilderness and culture.

For almost ten years I have been playing weekly games of Go with my friend Pete Schumer. Invented in China and refined in Japan, Go is a board game in which opponents alternate placing round, flattened stones on 361 intersections. White and black stones swirl around each other as the players contend for dominance over territory in various portions of the board. A pattern emerges in which the stones of both colors combine—a beautiful, intricate design beyond competition or intention.

Aji is a concept in Go that helps me understand the swirl of nature and wildness in Vermont. Sometimes a player turns away from an area of the board where the opponent's position has become dominant. But the seemingly abandoned stones retain *aji* within the opposing color's sphere of influence. This word, which comes from the Japanese term for a lingering "taste," describes the fact that a minimal presence can suddenly "come alive." Scattered, discounted stones are empowered, combining with new ones of the same color when the action spills back into that sphere after an engagement elsewhere. The little patches of wilderness in our state have functioned as a kind of *aji*. Wildness spreads back down into the Champlain Valley from rugged heights like Bristol Cliffs.

Go, with its circularity and suspension, reflects my experience of wilderness and culture in New England. What began as an opposition has slowly revolved into a balance. When I attended high school in California, I played a lot of chess. That's how the wilderness movement felt then, too. Double ranks of chessmen squared off for an apocalyptic encounter. Black and white lines clashed at the center of the board, and the number of pieces diminished until one side obtained the leverage to force checkmate. But the number of stones in Go increases steadily in a game. When all portions of a board have been tested and claimed or relinquished, the players decide that the game is at an end; there is no checkmate and, if the proper number of handicap stones was placed down at the beginning, the game is often within a few points of being a tie.

One reason why a Japanese metaphor appeals to me for the recovery of New England's wilderness is that both regions would be called the East in California. This paradox of directions on a round planet evokes for me another ancient symbol originating in China, which shows the creative forces of the cosmos as swimming shapes of dark and light that curve around to form a single circle. At the heart of the circle's darker side is a white dot, while a seed of blackness nestles in the light. *Aji*, an intricate pattern of complementarity and balance.

Just as areas like Bristol Cliffs have been saving remnants in Vermont, isolated patches from which the heights could once more grow toward wilderness, the plane on South Mountain is a different kind of redemptive trace. This wilderness will never be pristine again, any more than the shattered Helldiver will ever fly. The machine guns will not be dredged up from the muddy margins of the pond. But a dialogue between wilderness and culture is what we need now anyway, not a resolution. It may keep us from drawing our boundaries too straight, and remind us that sometimes we must go down before we find our second chance. The western-based environmental movement has often asserted the value of "virgin wilderness." But Vermont's return to wildness around the wreck offers, instead, the image of a marriage. Not a dichotomy, but a dynamic, procreative union.

When I first hiked up into Bristol Cliffs last August to find that plane, my image of the wreck screened out the world that I was passing by. Back home again on this December evening, though, when what I see is the glow of my computer's screen, and when what I hear is the steady current of its fan, I recall the late summer world I waded through, looking for something else.

Leaves were thick and dark overhead, making the forest a cool, flickering place. The warmth of decay had coaxed out mushrooms everywhere—dimpled and white, day-glo orange, and the spotted tan ones that are scattered around the stumps like toads. Stands of goldenrod and black-eyed susans grew in the clearings, but most of the woodland wildflowers were already gone by. In the dim light under the trees, only the whorled wood asters were still blooming, their limp white petals wreathed round the loose-packed yellow of the central disk—elegant late bloomers, lingering among the berries.

And berries there were: baneberries like little clusters of white pop beads, trilliums with their single, maraschino-bright fruit, clintonia with their pairs and triplets of purple berries turning black. Wildflowers lingered in their progeny, the consummation of their moving on. The August woods retained a memory of July. And now, as the earth undertakes its cold passage through December, orbiting back toward June, I return in writing to the scene of my reiterated hike. Memory compounds and thickens like the third-growth woods above my Bristol home.

Succession

As for the woods' excitement over you
That sends light rustle rushes to their leaves,
Charge that to upstart inexperience.
Where were they all not twenty years ago?
They think too much of having shaded out
A few old pecker-fretted apple trees.

After breakfast today I drove up the steep road along the New Haven River that Rita takes to her teaching at Lincoln School, then took a turn south on Briggs Hill Road and continued to a little pull-off at the eastern entrance to Bristol Cliffs Wilderness. This is the only access-point indicated with Forest Service road signs, the only place where one can park and hike off immediately into the Wilderness. Since being shown the trail that climbs past the talus slopes on the western side, I've rarely used this approach. But it was for several years the only way I knew how to get into Bristol Cliffs.

I paused after parking the car and looked east to Mt. Abraham, the patriarch that towers above the New Haven Watershed. While the snow here was still just four or five inches deep and no problem to tramp through, up on Abraham there were now drifts above waist-high. I snowshoed up to the summit eight days ago, on January 9th, to scatter my father's remaining ashes. All fall I'd been hiking with them in my daypack, looking for the most fitting place. But no spot felt right until I finally looked up to Mt. Abe. This is one of four mountains in Vermont that rise above tree-level, and all of it is pure white today—with a nubbly band showing where the prime fir and spruce give way to the krummholz's twisty miniatures, then a gleaming wash on the summit's final, tilted slabs of stone.

When I went up on snowshoes last week, it was just about 20 degrees, the same as today, and there was little wind. The main sound was the *chuff, chuff* of my shoes sinking into the snow—almost like the gusting impacts I hear over my shoulder when I toss back shovelfuls of dirt while trenching our garden in the spring or when digging a hole to plant a tree. In climbing Mt. Abe, I would also sometimes hear a sudden *whoomp* when a balsam bough released its densely packed load of snow, the careful balance disturbed by my passage. Even on top of the mountain, the air was unusually still and the sunshine felt warm to me after the ascent. I walked over to where I could look straight down at Deer Leap and Bristol Notch, with the village on the other side, and removed the little oval box of ashes from my pack. It was a bronze container that Rita and I had bought twenty-five years ago in Ghana. After I offered thanks for the beauty of my father's life and for the beauty of the day, I removed the lid and cupped the mouth of the box into a light breeze that had arisen. The ashes stirred and lifted, streaming out like smoke toward the northwest and home.

Recalling that moment, I turn now and enter this local wilderness, which holds familial memories of its own. When I was hiking in from this side regularly, in 1980 and 1981, I often brought our daughter Rachel, who was little more than a toddler. In those years, the old logging road we followed into the woods was a more distinct track, but we still never made much headway. Most of those hikes were in the summer and fall, and Rachel was fascinated by the density of both life and decomposition in this ungroomed world. The trail rolled up and down through a congregation of beech and maple, with ferns in profusion all along the way. On the western, rocky side of Bristol Cliffs, the boulders harbor Christmas ferns and common polypody—evergreens that look especially brilliant against the snow. But the ferns that predominate here on the eastern side—sensitive ferns, New York ferns, woodferns, and broad beech ferns—have shriveled and disappeared long before this morning. The only vestiges I see now are the little spore cases of the sensitive ferns, sticks that hold up their rows of hard, black, wrinkled berries. I can clearly picture the sensitive ferns' flattened, robust fronds, though, just as I can still see Rachel in my mind's eye—a four-year-old with her blonde hair pulled back by barrettes and the thick-lensed, pink-rimmed glasses that she wore because of a wandering eye, now long since corrected. One of her special delights was to find a log that, while still looking basically intact, was far enough decomposed to be pulled apart with her hands as she looked for grubs like a little bear.

Soon after entering Bristol Cliffs from this Lincoln side I come to a placard held up by a green metal post. Below the heading, "National Forest Wilderness," it reads "Closed to motor vehicles and motorized equipment," and under that it says "Area back of this sign is managed and protected under Public Law (16 U.S.C. 551; 16 U.S.C. 1131–1136)." What such protection finally means in this part of the East is not that something in particular will be *preserved,* so much as that certain kinds of human disturbance will be eliminated in order that *other* cycles of disturbance and transformation may churn along unimpeded in these woods.

The logging road comes abruptly to an end at the beaver pond where Rachel and I generally completed our forays and turned around. Light new snow covers the thin ice today and frosts the lodge that rises from the pond in an untidy mound of branches and twigs. The land drops down pretty steeply just below the horseshoe shape of the dam itself. Water sieves out and trickles down the length of the dam's stockaded wall. Giant beavers were wiped out at the start of the present interglacial period, while modern beavers, too, were just about driven extinct in the middle of the nineteenth century. Today, though, our beavers have recovered dramatically throughout the Northeast and are one of the major influences on the character of our forests.

Even within this period of recovery, though, there are cycles of occupation and abandonment at a given dam. Beavers rely exclusively on the bark, twigs, and leaves of hardwood trees for food, and when all the hardwoods have been gnawed down within a certain radius of one dam, they look for a promising new site. Scientists coring old dams have discovered that, after lapses of time allowing hardwoods to regenerate in the vicinity, such sites have been recolonized numerous times. There's commonly a thicket of speckled alders, with their multiple trunks and flecked, cherry-like bark, growing right around a beaver pond. Alders are successional opportunists, adapting well to the tides of water and light that determine the fluctuating fortunes of a colony.

I've always relied on the kindness of scientists, particularly as I've tried to read Vermont's cut-over and recovering woods. An especially helpful one has been Tom Wessels, who teaches field ecology at the Antioch Environmental Studies Program in New Hampshire. One of Tom's generalizations is that there are three factors determining the specific vegetation within a given "phytogeographic" region—the type of substrate, the elevation and exposure, and disturbance. The main kinds of disturbance determining what he calls the "successional history" of a site are in turn fire, logging, blowdowns, defoliation, beavers, and pasturing. Several of these are easy enough to read. No one could miss a beaver dam, and ancient, clean-cut stumps deep in the woods tell an indisputable tale of logging. In addition to charred stumps like my landmarks on the Cliffs trail, there are other reminders of past fires, too. When the basal scars of trunks face each other, they mark the edges of a logging road. But when they flicker on the uphill side of a whole slope of trees, they show where a forest fire climbed around them and ignited little piles of duff and twigs that had slid down over several seasons and piled against the trunks. Though the trees themselves may have survived the climbing wall of flames, a small conflagration lingered beside each one and scorched the bark for a few feet up.

Tom Wessels taught me several signs of previous pasturing, too. One is of course the existence of stone walls. Another is the presence of junipers, a slow-growing species easily choked out by grasses, and one that can thus only grow in environments like rocky ledges, mossy ground, and constantly cropped pastures. Finally, there are what Tom called "weird apples." Though they may be isolated now under a canopy of red maples, these apples would have often gotten their start amid or beside a pasture, where they were sometimes cropped by livestock into some pretty contorted shapes. Now, knotty, twisted, and riddled with holes, they have a feral look, as when boars assume new tusks and bristles upon forsaking the farmyard for the woods.

Frost, too, finds in weird apples a marker of how the New England woods have been transformed even within his own lifetime.

> As for the woods' excitement over you
> That sends light rustle rushes to their leaves,
> Charge that to upstart inexperience.
> Where were they all not twenty years ago?
> They think too much of having shaded out
> A few old pecker-fretted apple trees.

Frost's lines insist upon the relative newness of this dense forest, and are reinforced by the sarcastic mastery of his rhythms. The gusty lightness of "As for the woods' excitement over you / That sends light rustle rushes to their leaves" is achieved by a shift toward unstressed syllables, in lines that skip along with four main beats instead of the usual five. But the alliteration of "light" and "leaves," as well as of "rustle rushes," is a lyrical effect whose decorative quality is crunched in the following line—"Charge that to upstart inexperience." This kind of satirical comment about the woods feels odd. It's much more usual in poetry to find a reverential contrast between human transitoriness and the forest's immemorial life. But the speaker in "Directive" insists upon his own greater experience, almost as if saying, "Before the forests were, I am." The question that follows clenches this sense of *priority.* "Where were they all not twenty years ago?" He knows where *he* was. Frost himself can certainly remember, from his youth in Massachusetts and from his own work as a poultry farmer in the early part of the century, a time when New England was still dominated by a farm culture just beginning to fade into the shade of upstart trees.

But the superior tone of these lines also has a bitter edge, suggesting a view that is anything but serene and detached from the world of change. The need for a perspective transcending the latest disturbances might be related to Frost's own life in the years right before "Directive" appeared in 1946. His wife Elinor had died in 1938, and in the same year Frost had purchased the Homer Noble farm in Ripton. He lived in a cabin up the hill, while Theodore and Kay Morrison were in the main farmhouse as his summer tenants and, in effect, his caretakers. A visitor to the Frost cabin finds a simple three-room structure of peeled logs, suitable for a hermitage, or for a mourning man's retreat. Marriage had proven intense and sometimes unsettling for Robert and Elinor, including both passionate periods and grim, silent standoffs. But this relationship had always remained the focal point of his emotional life, and a central influence upon his choices as a poet.

His fierce possessiveness about Elinor, dating from their graduation at Lawrence High School as co-valedictorians in 1892, and his smoldering preoccupation with his poetry seem sometimes to have made living with Frost a burden. His own regrets in looking back over the long history of troubled love must have been sharpened by his daughter Lesley's outburst immediately after Elinor's death. According to Lawrance Thompson, she stormed that Frost had ruined her mother's life, and that she would never let him live with her, lest he oppress her children's growing up as he had the childhood of his own daughters and son.

Thompson's magisterial, if sometimes strangely hostile, biography of the poet supports the claim that he was a difficult husband and father—in Bernard DeVoto's words, "a good poet, but a bad man." In the index of Thompson's second volume *(Robert Frost: The Years of Triumph)*, there are sixty-five "topical sub-heads" under "Frost, Robert," with a striking prevalence of such negative, and sometimes derogatory, categories as "Anti-Intellectual," "Baffler-Teaser-Deceiver," "Brute," "Charlatan," "Cowardice," "Depression, Moods of," "Escapist," "Fear," "Gossip," "Hate," "Insanity," "Jealousy," "Misunderstanding," "Murderer," "Pretender," "Punishment," "Rage," "Self-Centeredness," "Spoiled Child," and "Vindictive."

Frost's correspondence with friends such as Louis Untermeyer often acknowledges how painful it could be to live with him, for himself as well as for others. Trying to stay afloat in the darkness of his own mind and heart may have been especially hard in the years between Elinor's death and the publication of "Directive." His son Carol, after a long struggle with mental illness, took his life in October of 1940. His daughter Irma was increasingly withdrawing into a world of phobias and anxieties, too, in ways that required more and more frequent intervention and support by her aging father. Her mental distress was all the more unsettling because it seemed to parallel so closely the degeneration of Frost's sister Jeanie, who had been institutionalized in the final years of her life. And overshadowing this decade that made Frost more than once liken his existence to Job's, there was of course the spectacle of a World War.

Unlike several of my senior colleagues at Middlebury, I never knew Frost personally. My own resistance to the extremely harsh view of him that might emerge from Thompson stems from two sources. One is my experience of the poetry's beauty and wisdom, while the other is the testimony of people like our college's Professor Reginald Cook and Rabbi Reichert, both of whom knew Frost very well and held him in the highest esteem. Rabbi Reichert is quoted in a recent book as saying that he didn't see how anyone who had been privileged to converse with the poet could then write about Frost without bringing in all of the *laughter*. I want to emphasize that my primary interest is in the poetry itself rather than in the biography of the writer. There can be no doubt that suffering and darkness are strongly evident in Frost's writing, too. But a poem like "Directive" finds beauty amid the dark thicket of loss and disconnection, or, rather, it affirms the place of darkness within the dynamic wholeness of life's beauty.

Lawrance Thompson's skepticism about Frost's character does not prevent him from being a highly perceptive reader of his poetry. Thompson connects the opening of "Directive," and its reference to "all this now too much for us," with another poem appearing with it in the volume *Steeple Bush*. "One Step Backward Taken" describes both the collapse of a hill under the onslaught of erosion and the kind of strategic retreat that can help one withstand a *personal* loss.

> Not only sands and gravels
> Were once more on their travels,
> But gulping muddy gallons
> Great boulders off their balance
> Bumped heads together dully
> And started down the gully.
> Whole capes caked off in slices.
> I felt my standpoint shaken
> In the universal crisis.
> But with one step backward taken
> I saved myself from going.

A world torn loose went by me.
Then the rain stopped and the blowing,
And the sun came out to dry me.

"Backward," and "back." Withdrawing just in time from a stand-point disappearing beneath his feet, the speaker finds a secure place to stand and wait it out as "[a] world torn loose went by me." The circle turns, the sun appears, and life continues. Thompson sees "One Step Backward Taken" and "Directive" as growing out of "the same sense of terrifying dislocation." He goes on to remark that "where the speaker in 'One Step Backward Taken' had saved himself *from* going by spatial retreat, salvation here [in "Directive"] is to be achieved *by* going—on a ritualized journey whose direction is backward in time, but also inward to levels of perception unaffected by external circumstances."

What I feel most grateful for in "Directive," though, is the way in which external circumstances *do* constantly transform and inform the internal ones, the way in which the landscape and the mind are mutually enriching for Frost. This is his greatest gift as a poet, his greatest gift to his readers—gifts of a world larger, more complex, and more dynamic than any idea, and toward whose always-elusive-because-always-renewing reality his own cagey poems aspire. The present book testifies to the ways in which "Directive" has been my best guide into the providential wilderness above our Bristol home. When Thompson discusses the poem that came right before "One Step Backward Taken" and "Directive" in *Steeple Bush,* which is called "Something for Hope," he comments that it contributes "to a thematic whole dominated not by secular but by spiritual concerns." But again, I want to quarrel with the dichotomy. In addition to celebrating patience and hope, as it certainly does, this poem chronicles with wonderful precision the biological cycle through which a meadow may turn first to a field and then to a forest, before being cut and used once more as a meadow.

In the first two stanzas of six in "Something for Hope," Frost writes,

> At the present rate it must come to pass,
> And that right soon, that the meadowsweet
> And steeple bush, not good to eat,
> Will have crowded out the edible grass.
>
> Then all there is to do is wait
> For maple, birch, and spruce to push
> Through meadowsweet and steeple bush
> And crowd them out at a similar rate.

No American poet has shown more familiarity than Frost with the cycles of plant succession in his own region. All of the fields around the Homer Noble farm would have long ago followed the trajectory of these two stanzas and reverted to thick woods, except for the fact that they are annually mowed, hayed, or burned by the Bread Loaf School of English or the Forest Service. These human disturbances are intended to maintain the particular kind of dynamic edge that prevailed in the Green Mountains during most of Frost's life.

Meadowsweet and steeplebush lift their blossoms above the tall grass throughout much of the summer. These two species of *Spiraea,* the former a lovely pale pink, the latter tending toward purple, rise waist-high on their sturdy stalks. Steeplebush calls for special attention, since it gives the entire volume of poetry its name. The little individual flowers, each with five petals, cluster into tall, fuzzy-looking arms of blossom that angle up sharply and form the spire. They bloom from the top down, with the upper clusters turning brown while the lower ones are still mellowing into a dark purple. The texture and color of the steeplebush are further enhanced as the season progresses by the fact that the tops of the serrated leaves remain green, while the undersides become a pronounced yellow. These striking flowers, mentioned in several poems by Frost, are the mid-way point in a cycle whereby a farmer's meadow is transformed, in the natural course of things, into a realm of trees. This hundred-year cycle is too long to be of economic advantage to any human individual, as the poet specifies. But it does offer a redemptive vision of inclusiveness, with each plant, from grass to maples, as well as the human onlooker, bound together in a dynamic whole. In Frost's landscape, things are always changing, but the change is never random. There is a grand logic of transformation, meaningful to the thoughtful observer, but always transcending the limited human purposes with which we might identify one phase or another of the whole.

The woods around this January beaver pond are a laboratory of succession—the pattern of continuity within change which was so central to Frost's perception of nature. Next to the pond, where logging seems to have occurred most recently, stands a dense grove of red maples. These large, attractive hardwoods often precede sugar maples in the reforesting of moist, disturbed ground. They are quite similar to those more familiar cousins, except for the V's between the sections of their leaves as opposed to the U's dividing the foliage of sugar maples. Yellow birches, smelling of wintergreen where little curls of bark peel off their trunks, are also mixed into these woods, as are a few ancient, slow-growing hemlocks.

On the other side of the pond, although there are few signs of logging, the ground is broken into a pronounced alternation of humps and hollows. Foresters call such a pattern of disturbed ground "pit and mound" or "pillow and cradle." It registers blowdown. When trees have toppled over, a half-circle of their roots tilts up into the air, exposing a hollow in the ground that remains even after the fallen log has begun to rot and the exposed roots have subsided into a softly contoured mound covered with soil and leaves. Our County Forester, David Brynn, counsels me always to think of

trees from the root-collar down. Remember, David says, that at least as much of a tree's biomass will generally be below the ground as is above it, with the root-circle of an old hemlock often spreading out for forty or fifty feet. Remember that even for the white pines which sink such a mighty taproot, an equal amount of root by weight is in the tiny filaments that spread their interwoven mat just below the topsoil's nutrient sink. Blow-down raises the hidden life of trees into the light.

I appreciate "pillow and cradle" as a phrase to describe this juxta-position of a depression in the woods and a nearby hump of raised ground. It expresses the perpetual renewal within the rise and fall of individual trees. Another eloquent term is "nurse log," describing the way in which a fallen tree nourishes seedlings along its length, making its stored energies available to the ongoing life of the forest. A fallen evergreen may decay, and nurse new life, over a period of sixty to seventy years, Tom Wessels informs me, while a hardwood log may decompose and make itself available within a cycle of thirty to fifty years. In his essay "Ancient Forests of the Far West," from *The Practice of the Wild,* Gary Snyder celebrates the nourishing per-sistence of fallen elders: "And then there are some long subtle hum-mocks that are the last trace of an old gone log. The straight line of mushrooms sprouting along a smooth ground surface is the final sign, the last ghost, of a tree that 'died' centuries ago."

A fallen log is something for hope. Not a hope for personal im-mortality, and not an assurance of prosperity or any other form of individual security. A hope, rather, for involvement in the grand pat-tern that connects. The southward orientation of many pillow-and-cradle formations in the rising ground just west of here tells of an-other event that occurred in 1938, along with the death of Elinor Frost and Robert's move into the little cabin at the woods' edge. A hurricane swept through this part of New England, absolutely level-ing thousands of acres. Pillows and cradles in identical alignment show me its tracks amid the trees of Bristol Cliffs. Seedlings quickly establish themselves in the full light and nutrient-rich litter of such a vast blow-down. In disaster, they have discovered grounds for hope.

⫸ I visited my father in Hillhaven Convalescent Home shortly before he died. His gaunt head was propped up on a lofty white pillow, and his arms looked thin and frail lying on top of the sheets. Looking at his arms, though, I thought of a day when I was a boy of six and he and I rowed a borrowed skiff way out into the Gulf of Mexico. The boat had been in storage for years, so that the bottom was dried out and leaky. Water began to well up, then suddenly rushed through the separating planks. Our boat sank with us too far from shore even to make out the white porch railings of our little vacation house. But my father calmly said to put my arms around his neck so that he could swim us in. I remember the total security I felt, resting on the smooth, powerful muscles of his back, watching the sweep of his arms through the brown water. I drowsed along, safe with my father above the invisible currents of the deep. I remembered that strength in Hillhaven, looking down at his thin arms and bony, age-spotted hands. I remember it now, in the life-and-death of this Vermont wilderness.

Death and life are both embodied in a nurse log. Nature is always unified for one who can let go and identify with a life that transcends individuality. But certain propositions are much easier to affirm in the abstract, and such letting go sometimes requires first being overturned and uprooted. Frost's first volume of poetry, *A Boy's Will,* was published in 1913. One stanza of "In Hardwood Groves" from that volume connects the need to fall back into the fund of life not only with blow-down but also with the annual descent of leaves.

> Before the leaves can mount again
> To fill the trees with another shade,

They must go down past things coming up.
They must go down into the dark decayed.

I feel Frost's struggle in the reiterated "must," as in the phrase "dark decayed." Decomposition at the bacterial level may be easier to contemplate if one leaves one's own body out of the picture. But only with an inclusive perspective on the universal breakdown of organisms can one look past it to new life. Only by adopting a time-line that comprehends the visitations of glaciers and the rise and fall of whole forests may one draw the lesson home. This is the tough but liberating view of life taught by the memory-tangled, ever-new New England woods.

Without Frost, it would have been much harder for me to appreciate the human meaning of these woods. Growing up in northern California, I was within a bike ride of Muir Woods. That grove of redwoods was my criterion for natural integrity as I began to enjoy nature on my own. When I eventually moved east to attend graduate school, the woods of Connecticut left me feeling disappointed and disoriented. They seemed to lack the sublime beauty of the redwoods with their grand columns rising through the filtered light, their forest floor almost devoid of underbrush. Walking in a little patch of forest near Guilford, Connecticut, I felt how small the trees were, how little they conformed to the monolithic simplicity of the redwoods, and how littered the forest floor felt with its broken branches and leaf-duff everywhere. I felt closed into a messy room rather than released into natural grandeur. Another grad student from the West repeated to me the libel, based on the relative smallness and proximity of landforms in this part of the country, that being in New England was like living in a teacup. Right, I thought, and in the tattered leaves that slid around my boots I'd found the dregs.

But Frost offers a vision of sublimity based not on spaciousness and noble clarity but rather on endurance in the face of loss, unity in fragmentation, and the warmth of decay. These are primarily physical truths for him, not metaphysical ones. Snow covers and temporarily arrests the decomposition of this forest floor, but beneath it lie the vestiges of several successive growing seasons. The top layer —"fit[ting] the earth like a leather glove," as Frost has it at the beginning of "In Hardwood Groves"—is composed of the brown but intact leaves of the previous fall. Beneath them is a layer of fragments and skeletons, sometimes just the spines of leaves, or the tips, or the outlines of maple or red oak leaves defining a webwork of holes. Just below those shards, and yet another year earlier, are found the crumbly little indistinguishable scraps, the chaff of three seasons' winnowing. And then comes the sweet black dirt. This soil is the "dark decayed," a layer of renewal from which sweet nutrients seep down into the mineral mix, food for the trees that hang overhead in familial continuity.

A forester named George Kessler introduced me to the concept of soil horizons. The decaying leaves and fragments mark the O, or organic, horizon, while the topsoil, lying beneath that fertile litter, is the A horizon. Below that comes the B horizon, or subsoil, which contains relatively little organic material. Slicing down into the forest floor, he showed me the lines of demarcation from the light brown of duff to the black of topsoil to the mineral-rich red-brown of the subsoil. New England, like the West, has its own big sky, but its horizons stretch beneath our boots. The circulation of water is like wind for this saturated soil. It bears leaves and ashes down through three horizons, then lifts them into trees that, even in early January, have their buds fully formed and ready to receive the spring.

As I began this year's long hike northward toward Bristol and home, a notable essay on Frost came out in the *New Yorker* of September 26, 1994. Joseph Brodsky's "On Grief and Reason" was impressive, as one strong poet's serious reading of another always is. But it also helped me understand my own reading of Frost more clearly, through certain reservations I felt about his. Brodsky says of the earlier poet that "on the surface, he looks very positively predisposed toward his surroundings—particularly toward nature. His fluency, his 'being versed in country things' alone can produce this impression." But unlike the inescapably *historical* reference that European poets bring to a foray out of doors, Brodsky writes,

> when an American walks out of his house and encounters a tree it is a meeting of equals. Man and tree face each other in their respective primal power, free of references: neither has a past, and as to whose future is greater, it is a toss-up. Basically, it's epidermis meeting bark. Our man returns to his cabin in a state of bewilderment, to say the least, if not in actual shock or terror.

In fact, though, nature *always* has a past, and an awareness of natural history includes and lifts up into coherence the history both of individuals and of humanity as a whole. Many writers have experienced America as an Eden, or a hell, of unnamed forms, just as Brodsky describes. But Frost is absolutely not one of them. He constantly reads the past within the present, and earns this large vision in part by encountering and admitting the disintegration of his own individuality. "Nature for this poet is neither friend nor foe, nor is it the backdrop for human drama; it is this poet's terrifying self-portrait," Brodsky writes. But his proposition, like Thompson's opposition between the spiritual and the secular, is built upon a false dichotomy. For Frost, at least, true self-portraiture must also depict one's place on earth. He would refute both the self-creating impulses of high Romanticism and the environmentalism of "vast, pristine, and untrammeled" lands removed from all human endeavors. Frost in this way anticipates our contemporary, Gary Snyder. For both writers, sublimity finally depends less upon spatial extent than upon temporal expansiveness.

As Brodsky says, Frost is often unsettled by nature, discovering within it the darkness of his own shadow. But Frost also looks intently at each of the dynamic forms in which he glimpses aspects of himself. He rarely just encounters a "tree," with "bark." More often, the tree is named: beech or maple, hemlock, pine, or larch, with its size, its profile against the sky, its moment in the cycles of foliage and succession specified within the poem. Frost seems at times almost overwhelmed by the concreteness and multiplicity of nature. As "In Hardwood Groves" shows, the ceaseless transformations of nature, like the human condition itself, can be "too much for us." But the tug of a diverse, living world always renews his poetry.

D. H. Lawrence expressed his admiration for Thomas Hardy in a way that also bears on Frost's poetry.

> This is the wonder of Hardy's novels, and gives them their beauty. The vast, unexplored morality of life itself, what we call the immorality of nature, surrounds us in its eternal incomprehensibility, and in its midst goes on the little human morality play, with its queer frame of morality and its mechanized movement; seriously, portentously, till some one of the protagonists chances to look out of the charmed circle, weary of the stage, to look into the wilderness raging round.

"Incomprehensibility" affirms the vastness and complexity of nature. Frost's woods, like Hardy's heath, offer the possibility for getting seriously lost when the merely human realm has become too much for us. "Directive," even in a moment when it mocks the "excitement" of Vermont's "upstart" trees, always acknowledges that incomparably larger natural processes are at work. Frost pays such close attention to the particular forms and lives amid the Green Mountains because they both disorient and reorient him, because they insist upon an enlarged frame of reference. He reads the story of a glacier in the erratics dotting Vermont's long central ridge. And he helps me, as I lift my boot across the hummock of a moldering root-circle, to bear in mind the cycles of a forest's buried life.

Hiking out to Briggs Hill Road, I compounded my boot prints from the way in, making them spread out like snowshoes as I slid back down to the present. I was also walking once more through my memories, occasioned by this road, of Rachel as a toddler, "not twenty years ago." The path bore me back down to the present world, in which she is a stylish, black-clad college student. Rachel slyly tests me when we ride together in the car by playing alternative and hard-core rock, as far from the Dylan and Beatles of my own college years as the littered forests of New England are remote from the redwood groves. Despite all the years since Rachel's childhood, though, I can always picture with perfect clarity how she was *then*—just as in looking at the deep blue clintonia berries of late summer I always have a superimposed image of their yellow lily-bells swaying beside the trail in June. In opening the car door now and sliding behind the wheel of a world in which my father is no longer alive, I can also still picture how he used to push Rachel on her Big Wheel when she was three or so. It was a comical scene, since his technique was to position an old golf club against the back of her vehicle so that he wouldn't have to bend over as he propelled her around the sidewalks for hour after patient, cheerful hour.

➤➤ And here I am back in Bristol, working in our barn as the afternoon of this long day draws to a close. A couple of shop-lights shine down, plugged into an outlet on the deck with a long orange extension cord. A kerosene heater roars at my back and almost keeps me from shivering. I am drawing beads of glue along the edge of slender cedar strips, bending them around station-molds that establish the tapering contours of a canoe, and stapling them onto these molds in order to clamp them together, edge to edge, while the glue dries. All year, as I have been pursuing my hikes, I have also been stealing hours to work on this wooden canoe, as a project honoring my father's memory. It's a task considerably beyond my experience or skills, and one I would have never taken on had it not been for a dream.

Last August Rita and I were taking a two-day vacation on the coast, having dropped Caleb off at his youth-orchestra camp in New Hampshire and on our way to pick up Matthew from a canoeing camp in Maine. It was a rare time to relax together, and we spent most of one day strolling along the harbor in Camden and poking around in shops. One bookstore had a large section on sailing and boat construction, and I became fascinated by the books on canoe building. The next night we were in Portland and decided to go out to dinner for our twenty-fourth anniversary. This was stretching it, since it was only August 19th and the actual date was the 30th. But we weren't likely to have another evening so spacious as the beginning of school approached, and we had heard about an elegant little restaurant in the old part of town, called Alberta's Seafood Grill. The meal was in fact wonderful, the atmosphere warm and inviting. But throughout a very happy evening tears kept rolling down my cheeks, to my total surprise. It seemed funny, really, just an overflow of love.

That night, when we returned to our motel on the outskirts of town, I had a dream as vivid as the image of a clintonia blossom beside a trail. In it, a sleek cedar-strip canoe was floating on the water. Its mellow reddish-golden color especially struck me, along with its name, the Tribute, written in calligraphic script along the right side of the bow. I walked closer to the shore by which it hung and looked down at the smaller letters of the inscription on the bow-deck. It read "JLE" and below that, "1918–94." Around these letters and numerals were wreathed the words "of the current to the source," with "source" coming right around to the circle's beginning and making one continuous phrase. I wrote this dream down in my journal and told Rita about it, realizing that it was a kind of memorial to my father, still alive in Hillhaven Convalescent but in sad decline because of the progression of his Alzheimer's. This new link between him and one of my favorite lines from "West-Running Brook" stirred me, since Dad had been much on my mind. The dream felt like an appropriate form of homage, but then it faded from my mind, like other nighttime revelations.

Two days later, having picked up Matthew, we pulled into our driveway in Bristol to find a message from my mother waiting for us. Dad had died on the evening of August 19th. Frost's poem of haunting gave me permission to believe Dad's spirit traveled to me that night in tears and a dream. But it also made me buy the book that told how such canoes were made, rig up a shop in our drafty barn, and begin to transform a long crate of wooden strips into the curved and symmetrical integrity of a hull. These thin, pliable planks, which I purchased from a marine supply company in Buffalo, have bead-and-cove edges—one convex and the other concave to hold the glue even when the strips wrap around a curve rather than joining in a plane. They make me think this evening of the pillow-and-cradle patterns of a forest floor—the juxtaposition of hummock and hole that tells the story of succession and that includes passing generations of trees in the present of a single slope.

At the farther end of North Mountain lies Bristol Pond, my favorite spot for canoeing. Building this craft, I have both remembered my father and imagined paddling the completed Tribute across the pond on a placid summer day. That would bring some closure to this year of grieving, as well as to the reading, hiking, and writing that have flowed together in this book. It would be a chance to reflect in quietness, after the effort and disorientation of the trail. But now I must bend back over the canoe's skeleton and partial hull, stretching my arms out as far as they'll go to hold a new strip of the curve firmly in place while I set a couple of staples near the craft's stern. As my stapler clacks, a sudden gust rattles the big barn doors. The kerosene heater gives a roar, bathes the canoe for a moment in its vivid glow, then dies back down.

Someone's Road Home

GILMORE POND TO ROCKY DALE
FEBRUARY 9, 1995

> Make yourself up a cheering song of how
> Someone's road home from work this once was,
> Who may be just ahead of you on foot
> Or creaking with a buggy load of grain.
> The height of the adventure is the height
> Of country where two village cultures faded
> Into each other. Both of them are lost.

➤➤ At 6:30 the thermometer on our south porch showed three degrees above zero. I layered up with two wool shirts and a sweater and started hiking from Gilmore Pond soon after breakfast on this glacial day, intending to snowshoe the length of Bristol Cliffs Wilderness. The total distance on the map is just about three and a half miles, but they must be the world's longest miles. Ridges and gorges break up the line of sight in every orientation, meaning that I will have to consult my compass constantly while bushwhacking back and forth. The topo map shows that after the first mile I will be walking generally downhill as I make my way north toward the village of Bristol. But, even though starting out with every intention to obey the law of gravity, I know I'll still be required, like the New Haven River, to reverse my course again and again before arriving home.

The falling flakes are fine and hard at this temperature, spangling as they drift in the early light. If the temperature were just a few degrees lower, it probably wouldn't be snowing at all. As it is, these bright motes filter through the still air with the leisurely side-to-side of silt where a river delta debouches into the sea. Under the sort of wet, heavy snowfalls that come in March, the limber evergreen boughs will grow more and more massively caked with white, until the moment arrives when they will suddenly shrug it all off with a *whump*. By contrast, some of the thick lower branches of sugar maples and beech will invariably crack and unhinge under the spring snow's freight. But in this extreme cold the tiny rigid crystals, sifting down all night, have simply compacted closely as they alighted and have never shifted, however tilted the surface on which they landed.

Where fallen trunks slant across my path, graceful seven-inch-high walls of snow rung along on top of the gray wood. The flakes have aligned with one another to form a rippling texture reminiscent of the Southwest's finely grained sandstones. That region's redrock records hundreds of millions of years of sedimentation. Leaning against a cliff, you can feel on your palm the rasp of the past. Here, the walls and drifts of white register the sedimentation of just one night. They could all be gone before the week is out, liquefying into the magma of the thawing forest floor. But for this morning at least, the snow enjoys its own mineralized stability. Where one snow-laden ash falls in front of me just at eye-height, I impulsively push the basket of my ski-pole through the white surface, just above the line of its joining with the dark gray, furrowed bark. Immediately, I regret this violation of the hours' quiet endeavor. When withdrawing my pole, though, I also find that a perfect, arching hole remains within the otherwise undisturbed face of snow. I look through it at a world of whitening boles and branches, magnified by the stillness and by the ceaseless glinting of the flakes. Window Rock.

As in the larger geological processes making Bristol Cliffs what it is, there is a dynamic of loss and gain within this snowfall. Once more I've begun by walking on a vestigial logging road, reconciled to losing the track pretty soon in the resurgent woods, and proceed-

ing as usual by trial and error. But I've also been surprised by the way in which this snow, in more smoothly whitening the clearer and more level ground, has lifted the old road bed into renewed visibility. For this first part of the hike, at least, I can proceed confidently, almost as if the past several, obscuring decades had not happened.

> Make yourself up a cheering song of how
> Someone's road home from work this once was,
> Who may be just ahead of you on foot
> Or creaking with a buggy load of grain.

Freud once wrote that the neurotic repeats instead of remembering. Frost might be more skeptical than his Viennese contemporary about shedding much light on the soul's darkness, but he does share Freud's desire to advance toward wisdom through a vigorous effort of memory. The poet's particular emphasis is not so much upon our individual stories of childhood as it is upon remembering the origins of everything we see *around* us, in the tidal landscape of Vermont. The grooves in ledges speak of the ice that was the past, and will be the destiny, of this mountain range. Old logging roads that serve us now were all the more serviceable, and necessary, for the ancestors whose songs we must now make up.

"Make yourself up a cheering song" exemplifies Frost's tone at this point in the poem—dark, yet resolute, ironic, but also friendly. It conveys a mocking acknowledgment that a reader straggling around in broken country and thickety woods may need some cheering up now. Once again, the poem reminds me of the Freudian definition of an "illusion." In *The Future of an Illusion*, Freud defines this as what someone believes not because of any particular evidence, but rather because of a compelling psychological *need* to believe it. The made-up song in these lines does begin with the real *traces* of a road, but it makes a dramatic leap of faith in promoting that vestigial trail to "[s]omeone's road home from work." The idea of a road leading home is certainly a cheering one. But the road and the home still belong to someone else, whose name we don't even know.

The tenuousness of this cheer comes out in the word "may": "Who may be just ahead of you on foot / Or creaking with a buggy load of grain." Someone *may* be just ahead, but even in Frost's day the hill-farmers suggested by these lines had been gone for decades. The word "buggy" insists upon the anachronism, while the image of grain being carted *up* into the mountains emphasizes the precariousness, and the brief duration, of agriculture in such terrain.

Unless. Frost's cheering song is an illusion unless a reader's time-frame expands to take in both the glaciers and the farmers who arrived and departed along the grooves left by those moving walls of ice. The broader our perspective, the more immediately present do our ancestors in the land become. When an illusion is engaged with sufficient imaginative energy, then it may take on the power of Saint Paul's "faith": "the substance of things hoped for, the evidence of things not seen." For the past to become so personally real, one must experience a sort of breakdown, like Paul's on that other road, to Damascus. One set of rational categories collapses as a vaster order is suddenly perceived.

Frost's language in "Directive" is never more reverberant than in the cadence that follows here: "The height of the adventure is the height / Of country where two village cultures faded / Into each other." Each word has a special weight within the poem and within the topography of this morning's hike. "Height," repeated in a single line to give it a special emphasis, locates me here atop this crowning ridge of the Hogback Anticline. The long climb is over, and it's time to do some exploration of high ground that's anything but a plateau. As I look back over my shoulder at the snowshoes' crisp, overlapping outlines in the smoothed-out logging road, there seems to be new clarity in my course through the woods and into the poem. Such confidence will melt with next week's thaw, and with the next modulation of "Directive"'s tone. But as I stand here, warm from the climb and enjoying the sensation of my cheeks being caressed by falling ice as fine as mist, I see a new landscape of possibility. "Adventure" distills this moment in the excursion—such a positive word after the recent underbrush of "haunt," "ordeal," and "inexperience." Yet this note of promise is a confirmation, not a new suggestion. Even in the earlier moments of working and disorientation, Frost's energy and assertiveness have insisted that following him will not *only* be an ordeal. It is ultimately a quest.

It initially comes as a surprise when "height" and "adventure" are juxtaposed with "country" and "cultures" in the following line. The word "country" tends to be associated with flatter, more fertile lands, like those rolling westward toward Lake Champlain. "Culture" can suggest the arts, society, and an urban experience distinct from the adventure and solitude of wilderness. Again, though, Frost points out the connections that emerge if we entertain a longer time-line. He shows that traces of human industry and society, even of human longing, may be read among these hills—faded, yet vivid to a sympathetic eye. Just as it has smoothed the old logging road from Gilmore Pond into renewed visibility, last night's powdery snow has highlighted stumps, wind-throw, and the edge of an old clear-cut just to my east. A bright, white light outlines all differences—of pine and maple, boulder and underbrush—and enhances my ability to spot the ever-changing details of the woods. The earlier inhabitants of these mountains, along with their farms and fields and the roads that brought them home, live on in this morning's dynamic landscape. It's hard to bear our predecessors always in mind. But doing so might have helped avoid the bitter controversy of twenty years ago. That was when this snowy vantage-point and the surrounding several thousand acres were established as a congressionally protected wilderness.

➤➤ The history of Bristol Cliffs Wilderness Area is as bewildering and complex as its topography. The Wilderness Act of 1964 was inspired most directly by the National Parks and National Forests of the West. The first wildernesses designated were enormous tracts of land, often contiguous to more heavily used portions of the Parks and Forests, but largely unmarked by roads or settlements. In these areas, back-country hikers could travel in solitude for days or weeks, encountering abundant wildlife and exploring forests, rivers, and mountains that seemed, well, pristine. As a Californian coming east for graduate school and never expecting to remain here, I was struck not only by the relative smallness and closeness of the mountains but also by the steady pressure of history on my experience of the woods. This region felt like a diminishment for the first few years, until I gradually became aware of the natural, historical, and aesthetic *thickness* of the landscape. The dramatic seasons of Vermont seemed to heighten, and even to lengthen, the year. The leaves and leaf-meal through which my hiking boots scuffed drew my attention downward to the growth of soil, just as the deliberate progression of my snowshoes emphasizes each step today. This is a landscape, in all seasons, that repays attentiveness to footing. The old roads and bottles and piles of stone scattered beneath the pines and hemlocks of our ridge always remind me that I am not Adam after all, just as the sounds of chainsaws and traffic I could hear from Route 116 almost the whole way up insisted that this hike would not take place in Eden. These are healthy reminders, encouraging me to understand wilderness as an experience including family and work, rather than as an idyll or escape. It was to celebrate and protect just such little patches of wilderness in the midst of human settlement that the Eastern Wilderness Act of 1975 was passed by Congress.

The framers of this legislation began by acknowledging that there was little land east of the Mississippi that could qualify as wilderness by the standards used in the West. Roads were generally much closer together back here, for one thing. But even though, with the exceptions of Maine and upstate New York, wild areas were measured in the thousands of acres rather than the hundreds of thousands of the West, there were still areas of great beauty and diversity within the more densely populated East. Accordingly, eighteen little pocket-wildernesses were established by Congress, one of them being Bristol Cliffs. If the 1975 Act was something of a stretch, by previously established standards for wilderness, Bristol Cliffs may have been the single instance where Congress most over-extended itself. Because the original area of approximately 7,000 acres included about 2,500 acres of private property and fourteen homes, its establishment caused a local controversy. The outcome —after a year of bitter protest—was a new Act of Congress focused exclusively on little Bristol, and in which, for the only time in our nation's history, acreage was withdrawn from a federally designated wilderness area.

In retrospect, at least, the history of that controversy can be read in the topo map I carry with me in a transparent case on this morning's expedition. Unfolding it awkwardly with my deerskin mittens, I confirm that the original land protected by Bristol Cliffs Wilderness Area was almost identical to a rugged parallelogram of land lying between the main roads. Route 116 established the original area's western boundary before turning sharply east to retrace the New Haven River's passage through Bristol Gap. The eastern border was the road to Lincoln, climbing to the south from 116 as it follows the river's gorge even further up the mountain. Finally, along the southern edge ran Upper Notch Road, which served to connect 116 to Forest Road 294 and then to the Lincoln Road.

But only about half of this roadless polygon is today still marked off as wilderness area. This is primarily the acreage, shaded in governmental green on my map, that already belonged to the National Forest. The white portions, mostly in the lower part of the polygon and immediately along Route 116, were private holdings—including a few year-round residences and a number of woodlots—that were in effect condemned by the legislation. The Forest Service declared itself ready to buy people's newly enclosed land at a fair price, but in the meantime issued warnings against unlicensed cutting of trees or other actions with an impact on the natural environment. As these restrictions became more widely understood, a Bristol Cliffs Landowners' Association was formed in protest. To many people in the surrounding towns it felt like a land-grab, just another case of Big Government intruding upon people's private lives and property. One landowner, Greta Vincent, wrote to the *Valley Voice* on July 2, 1975, of her outrage at the intention of "the government [to] come in and take over, which they are not going to do to our home. We will fight one way or another because us *back woods people* wouldn't know any other way to do."

The Landowners' Association was not only irate but also politically effective. Between summoning Senators Leahy and Stafford and Congressman Jeffords to Bristol for public hearings and sending a delegation down to Washington, D.C., they kept the pressure on until follow-up legislation specifically excluded from the Wilderness Area all private property originally contained in Bristol Cliffs. Although I lived in East Middlebury when this controversy was raging, rather than in Bristol, I can testify that extremely strong feelings linger from it today—feelings of triumph over what was viewed as a tyrannical bureaucracy, as well as simmering resentment about the attempted expropriation.

On July 14, 1979, I attended a follow-up hearing held in Middlebury. This one was a session of the Senate's Committee on Agriculture, Nutrition, and Forestry, called to solicit public input on establishing additional wilderness areas in Vermont's roadless areas. It thus provided an occasion for interested parties from around the state to revisit the Bristol Cliffs controversy. Members of the Bristol Landowners' Association had originally insisted that they were all for wilderness, as long as it did not imply any infringement of their rights. But by the time of this new hearing, feelings had hardened. Many people began by attacking the idea of wilderness, and the word itself, even if it were to be established entirely within the bounds of the National Forest. The philosophical issue on which many, like Seeley Reynolds of Salisbury, focused was utility. To let trees decay unharvested seemed to them a depressing waste:

> The proponents of more wilderness areas . . . want to leave a dark, dismal, dying, rotting, damp, non-efficient mature forest with no wildlife for future generations. I ask you, gentlemen, Haven't we left enough tragedy to future generations already? Let's leave a legacy, in Vermont at least, of young, fast growing, life-abundant, often-harvested forests which are fire protected, have cover and food for wildlife, and are, because of multiple use, made available to all of the Vermont public.

It was also common for people opposed to more wilderness areas to begin by establishing their credentials as true Vermonters. Mr. Reynolds, in one of his earlier statements at the hearing, had spoken of the ten generations of his own family in this part of Vermont.

> The first one was the first woman in the Champlain Valley, Ann Reynolds Story. Her husband was killed by a 4-foot tree in a mature forest, building his cabin. She finished the job with five kids and made her living by—listen to this; we all did it then, or they did it—cutting the trees down and burning them for the potash that they could lug on their back to Albany, N.Y.—the only resource of cash they could get those days.

Some of those in favor of establishing more wilderness areas soon felt compelled to admit that they were *not* Vermonters of many generations' standing. Ray Mainer of Hinesburg prefaced his own remarks by saying, "I wasn't born on a farm, and my ancestors weren't killed by falling trees." But, even though he couldn't draw on the venerable authority of his Vermont ancestors as Seeley Reynolds did, Ray Mainer was like him in focusing on the question of what sort of environmental legacy our children would be inheriting.

These roadless areas are now sort of going back to wilderness. Once 100 percent of Vermont was wilderness. We've lost 99 percent of it. We've got 1 percent left, or so we are told. Wilderness is not really a renewable resource. Once this has been declared open for development, that's it. Bingo. We probably will never have another chance. At least it won't be renewable within our lifetime, probably even your children's lifetime.

Wilderness is important to my life. I sort of make my living from wilderness. Every day I deal with cranky customers, obnoxious machines, smelly motors, everything. Every now and then I have got to get away from this, or I just won't be able to work. I need it to survive. It's what makes my work possible, and I hope that all these areas will be made wilderness.

When I sat in the audience for these hearings almost sixteen years ago, my sentiments were all on the side of the wilderness advocates. In the intervening period of living in Vermont and hiking Bristol Cliffs, however, my feelings have become more complicated. I still celebrate the establishment of six more wilderness areas as a result of those Middlebury hearings. But I also understand more clearly how people might have objected on a philosophical and ethical basis to that process I felt so good about. The historical realities now seem to me a terrain as rugged as the Hogback Anticline itself, and I make my way across by sharp switchbacks of sympathy.

What excites me about the establishment of wilderness areas like this one I'm snowshoeing through today is that it celebrates Vermont's dynamic of renewal through loss. Despite all the grandeur of the West's huge and dramatic wilderness, there always seemed a certain fatalism in the assumption that wilderness was an irreplaceable, and perpetually eroded, resource. If the language of the post-1964 wilderness movement sometimes implied that civilization was cancer, then the only chemotherapy to halt its spread would be restriction of the human population. I rejoice in the wildernesses that have been protected, from 1964 through the Alaska Lands Act of 1980, and also strongly agree that reducing the rate of population growth should be a priority for environmentalists. But a certain self-loathing can be implied by the assumption that people are the problem, and this is still a real difficulty with many expressions of the wilderness-ethic. Another way to put it is that humanity has sometimes been viewed as taboo with relation to wilderness—not only people but, in the emphasis upon roadless and "untrammeled" areas, our human history. The example of Vermont, however, shows that wilderness can grow as well as erode, and that the record of human activity can enrich nature's meaning. The logging road marked by impressions of my snowshoes leads me both into the wilderness and into the "cheering song" of predecessors I might not have imagined otherwise. Ancestors always accompany me on these hikes in Bristol Cliffs.

I think that the Forest Service got into so much trouble including private holdings within the original boundaries of Bristol Cliffs because of an assumption that the experience of wilderness, even that of a *recovered* wilderness like this one, was essentially ahistorical—or even "prehistoric." But in fact there were people within that green line, with their own firm sense of being the inheritors of earlier "backwoods people" amid the mountains of Vermont. The expression "living memory" beautifully expresses the standing integrity of a forest, but it also describes the sense of familial continuity that motivated some members of the Bristol Landowners' Association. The recovery of forest land is thrilling to those who have seen the massive deforestation in more populous sections of the country. By contrast, the maintenance of a few houses amid those woods affirms a certain cultural continuity for people whose ancestors settled here last century, when Vermont was much less forested. Cloise Baslow wrote to the paper as a person whose family had long lived within the Bristol Cliffs area. The importance of maintaining his home where it was came from his sense of rooted lineage: "My grandparents cleared the land in Bristol Notch and built their cabins and barn. My father and mother built a log cabin to live in when they were married. My mother fed any stray cat, dog, or person that came by her door and was hungry." Like Mr. Reynolds, he modeled his values on a tradition of cultivation and use. "My father is 91 years young, has lived with me for the past few years, and still digs holes, plants, hoes, and takes care of his garden." Such residents of the mountains responded to the establishment of the wilderness area by retorting, in effect, "Someone was already there." Or, as Frost put it, this was "someone's road home."

Joseph Conowal, who was generally considered the leader of the Bristol Cliffs Landowners' Association in their effort to have private lands excluded from the new wilderness area, developed this argument about priority in a telling form in his own letter to the editor of the *Valley Voice*. "Try doing something American for a good gesture in the Bicentennial year, admit you are wrong by giving the land back to the Indians for once: that is, the Bristol, Lincoln tribes." He glossed this analogy in another statement published at about the same time: "and by Indians, I mean us, the landowners."

Two things strike me about this likening of the embattled landowners to Indians. It dramatized the sense that local, rooted people like Mr. Baslow were being displaced by outsiders who were, in turn, backed by a colonizing government and its bureaucracies. To speak of "the Bristol, Lincoln tribes" was to express a belief that these landowners belonged—that their houses and gardens were not extraneous to the character and value of South Mountain. The longer our family lives in Bristol, the more sympathy I feel for others whose stories have connected them with this particular place on earth. Such an emphasis is also compatible with Frost's own interest in the "village cultures" that flourished in these highlands. "Directive" makes them more visible to newcomers like myself, arriving in this scrappy, providential wilderness from elsewhere.

Mr. Conowal's figure of speech brings up another complicated issue, however. Both the Landowners' Association and Frost date their human history from European settlement of Bristol in the late eighteenth century. But there were people here long before the current "Bristol, Lincoln tribes." They were the Western Abenaki, or People of the Dawn, who lived primarily in Vermont and Quebec. In the preface to their 1981 book *The Original Vermonters: Native Inhabitants Past and Present,* William Haviland and Marjory Power discuss the odd but common denial of a Native presence here. Even in the case of history texts, "most books on Vermont simply repeat one or another version of the old myth that Indians never lived in the state." The scanty references to the Abenaki in Robert Frost's poetry of rural Vermont, and the total absence of any such notice in "Directive," reflect a common disregard among the non-Native community in the decades leading up to 1946—even though numerous farmers, loggers, and other country people still traced their own ancestry back to the Abenaki. Frost's poem "The Vanishing Red" shows that he did at least recognize the competitiveness and hostility which led settlers in New England to suppress the very existence of their predecessors in this landscape. In the 1970s, though, Vermont saw a strong reassertion of indigenous presence and prerogatives in Vermont. That is when, as Haviland and Power put it, the Abenaki decided it was time to "go public." Just as the Bristol landowners confronted the Forest Service with a human reality that set back their design for wilderness, so too these "Original Vermonters" complicate "Directive"'s narrative of "two village cultures."

Frost does an extraordinary job of synthesizing the Western literary tradition, the history of European settlement in Vermont, and the geological background that determined the rise and fall of farms amid the heights. Especially given his ambition for comprehensiveness within "Directive," though, it's important to register his lack of attention to Abenaki history. This is a gap not just for the poem, but for American wilderness-thought in general. In the West, the emphasis upon pristine, Edenic wilderness arose in writ-

ers like John Muir who themselves resisted integrating the long
history of indigenous peoples into their vision. I have no desire to
downgrade Muir—a courageous conservationist and a writer of real
power. A photograph of him, sitting on a rock beside the Merced
River, hangs on my wall. However, even though Muir moves into
a more thoughtful phase later in his career when he encounters
Native peoples in Alaska, one cannot avoid the fact that his response to Mono Indians in his beloved Yosemite is dismissive and
racist:

> At length, as I entered the pass, the huge rocks began to close
> around in all their wild, mysterious impressiveness, when sud-
> denly, as I was gazing eagerly about me, a drove of gray hairy
> beings came in sight, lumbering toward me with a kind of bone-
> less, wallowing motion like bears.
>
> I never turn back, though often so inclined, and in this particular
> instance, amid such surroundings, everything seemed singularly
> unfavorable for the calm acceptance of so grim a company. Sup-
> pressing my fears, I soon discovered that although as hairy as bears
> and as crooked as summit pines, the strange creatures were
> sufficiently erect to belong to our own species. They proved to be
> nothing more formidable than Mono Indians dressed in the skins
> of sage-rabbits. Both the men and the women begged persistently
> for whisky and tobacco, and seemed so accustomed to denials that
> I found it impossible to convince them that I had none to give.
> Excepting the names of these two products of civilization, they
> seemed to understand not a word of English; but I afterward
> learned that they were on their way to Yosemite Valley to feast
> awhile on trout and procure a load of acorns to carry back through
> the pass to their huts on the shore of Mono Lake.
>
> Occasionally a good countenance may be seen among the Mono
> Indians, but these, the first specimens I had seen, were mostly ugly,
> and some of them fairly hideous. The dirt on their faces was fairly

stratified, and seemed so ancient and so undisturbed it might almost possess a geological significance. The older faces were, moreover, strangely blurred and divided into sections by furrows that looked like the cleavage-joints of rocks, suggesting exposure on the mountains in a cast-away condition for ages. Somehow they seemed to have no right place in the landscape, and I was glad to see them fading out of sight down the pass.

For Muir, to discover that his trail through Mono Pass was "someone's road home" was profoundly threatening. Similarly to the original proclamation-boundary for Bristol Cliffs Wilderness, his personal excitement about the Range of Light allowed "no right place in the landscape" for his predecessors. A striking feature of this denunciation is that, although Muir's likening of the little band he meets to Sierra animals seems intended to deny their humanity, such derogatory comments also imply, despite themselves, the Monos' greater identification with Yosemite. Theirs, after all, is a diet based on native acorns and trout, as opposed to Muir's dependence upon bread crumbs and tea brought up from the lowlands. Such closeness to nature is an uncomfortable reminder of how far he still has to go before this road will be his own.

To find a personal connection with the Bristol Cliffs Wilderness requires entering into the larger current of energies that swirl through this place. It means remembering both the glaciers that shaped these mountains and the farmers whose stone walls still linger among the trees. But it also means educating ourselves about the Native peoples who lived here, and who remain today even as an industrial society enacts itself along the highways of our state. Gary Snyder has dedicated considerable creative effort to understanding how settlers who want to belong more closely to a place are related to our Native predecessors. There is an inescapable difference between these groups. Yet walking the land and perceiving its seasons more sharply may still lead those of us who are immigrants to our

own deep sense of identification with a place, and with its indigenous cultures. Snyder constantly tries to keep the map of his local
drainages in mind as he goes about his daily life.

> Why should we do this kind of visualization? Again I will say: it
> prepares us to begin to be at home in this landscape. There are tens
> of millions of people in North America who were physically born
> here but who are not actually living here intellectually, imagina-
> tively, or morally. Native Americans to be sure have a prior claim
> to the term native. But as they love this land they welcome the
> conversion of the millions of immigrant psyches into fellow "Na-
> tive Americans." For the non-Native American to become at home
> on this continent, he or she must be *born again* in this hemisphere,
> on this continent, properly called Turtle Island.
>
> That is to say, we must consciously fully accept and recognize
> that this is where we live and grasp the fact that our descendants
> will be here for millennia to come. Then we must honor this land's
> great antiquity—its wildness—learn it—defend it—and work to
> hand it on to the children (of all beings) of the future with its
> biodiversity and health intact.

Earlier this afternoon, I crossed Bristol Cliffs' highest point.
It's a wooded knob just 2,325 feet above sea level, but the surrounding terrain is so irregular and fissured that snowshoeing up it
felt like a major ascent. Now, without even the vestige of a log-road
in sight, I'm trying to hold to an angle north and just a shade toward
the northwest. The land drops off sharply to my left, and I can look
across the tops of hemlocks rooted in blue-green clusters amid the
prevalent deciduous groves. They mark the drop-offs, beside which
the hemlocks strike their roots and into which they lean. I am attempting as I move forward now to follow Snyder's advice and visu-
alize the wholeness of my home watershed.

So much water is arrested all around me, in the snow beginning to pile up more thickly, in the heavy rime-ice packing the boughs of fir atop the knob, and in the frozen, yellow waterfalls that loom on the western-facing cliffs. But within two months a series of thaws will begin, first releasing barely liquid trickles and then propelling brown freshets down the slopes to the east, north, and west of my present route. An amazing fact is confirmed by my topo map, which I've just refolded to show the northern portion of Bristol Cliffs and the village. Though the water will radiate in every direction but due south from the part of the ridge where I'm now walking, it will all be reunited in the New Haven River. The river is curved around the wilderness area like a companionable arm, with its biceps in Lincoln, its elbow in Bristol's Rocky Dale, its forearm stretching out through New Haven, and its hand pointing up Otter Creek to the lake. This watery arc symbolizes what Aldo Leopold called the Round River—the circulation of water and life throughout the ever-renewing wholeness of the land.

Ever since my path started to descend, I have spotted an unusual number of standing snags—spruces, twisted and bleached pale gray, as well as funky old maples and yellow birches that gape with woodpecker holes. Such dead trees particularly catch my eye today because I have just read an article in the current *Natural History* called "Waves in the Forest." In it, Peter Marchand describes "fir waves," a phenomenon found only in the mountains of Japan and in the higher elevations of our American Northeast. To a hiker in the midst of such forests, the effect would be imperceptible within the general variety of tree-growth. From an aerial perspective, however, the pattern is striking and consistent:

> Crescent-shaped bands of dead and dying trees appear to advance through the forest, leaving vigorous saplings in their wake. Behind this dieback front, the age and height of these survivors gradually increase until the regenerating stand "crests" at the next line of

dead trees. Speeded up by time-lapse photography, the dying and regenerating forest would appear to be moving in waves. Each crest is separated by perhaps 300 feet and, in real time, takes 35 to 100 years to arrive at any given point. This is the shortest cycle of natural forest succession of which I am aware.

The clearest examples of fir waves in our region are at higher elevations than this—on Whiteface to my west in the Adirondacks or in the Franconia Range and on Katahdin to the east. But they also appear on Mt. Abraham and our other principal Vermont peaks, and do a great deal to explain the character of a recovered forest like this one at Bristol Cliffs. Just as these waves compress the process of forest succession, so too does the environmental history of Vermont illuminate the constant change of our resilient, water-rich region. The last word in the seven lines of "Directive" that frame this present excursion is "lost." When Frost last used that word in the poem, his reference was to his reader and hiker's imminent danger (or opportunity) of losing the *way*. But at this point in the poem it refers to the way "two village cultures" lost their very *place* in the land. Fir waves show that such loss need not indicate a contest for dominance or a linear progression. Rather, it may be a continual return of resources to the fund from which new life springs. Marchand writes of how trees which are exposed to wind and pests at the unprotected edge of a wave soon die, given the already severe stresses of such an extreme climate: "To the individual tree, the result is, of course, disastrous. To the aging forest as a whole, however, the process has a more positive effect. Nutrients that have been tied up for decades in the wood of the trees are released, sunlight reaches the understory once more, and a host of other organisms flourish before the canopy is closed again by the dominant species."

Frost would have relished the image of death and regeneration sweeping across the mountains like waves on the ocean. He understood well the principle of such succession, which he summed up in his poem "Something for Hope" as "A cycle we'll say of a hundred years." He could look with equanimity at the woods spilling over the meadows of old farms around him in Ripton, because he could see the larger process that contained and connected these vegetative phases, and understood the benefit to humans who could patiently contemplate a story longer than their own individual span of life. The poem's first two stanzas, quoted earlier, foresee the progression through meadowsweet to trees. The third and fourth stanzas counsel patience in the simple, cheerful voice one might use in calming down a fretful child.

> No plow among these rocks would pay.
> So busy yourself with other things
> While the trees put on their wooden rings
> And with long-sleeved branches hold their sway.
>
> Then cut down the trees when lumber grown,
> And there's your pristine earth all freed
> From lovely blooming but wasteful weed
> And ready again for the grass to own.

Though the principles of succession can sometimes be most visible from the air, they are also discernible for one like Frost, who stoops down to look at shoots newly sheltered amid the "wasteful weed." They are at work throughout this winter, too, both in the life fostered by hollow trees and in the upturned root circles, registered as humps beneath the snow.

The day has warmed gradually and has now reached something like 15 degrees above zero. As that has happened the flakes have fallen faster and blanketed the trees more sprawlingly. Even so, the new life springing from these dead trunks is inescapable. The largest snag I see on my current switchback to the east is barkless, and has just two remaining branches—probably an ancient birch, though I can't tell for sure. Numerous holes show where woodpeckers have probed it for the insects' nurseries. Gray circles of lichen blotch the trunk above snow line, and new soil has accumulated black and sweet in all its clefts. A tree well wrapped in its own snug bark would not foster so much new life, just as a ridge still settled, cleared, and fenced would not allow for this day's wandering adventure. The loss of one good thing may be the start of something else, as long as that wave, too, comes to its crest and slides on through.

Bristol Cliffs marks the loss of one vision of wilderness and the birth of a new one. But like the New Haven River wrapping around its rocky promontory, this progression is circular. My sense that Frost gives voice to the land's cycles is strengthened by the similar insights of another Vermonter. I often thought of George Perkins Marsh when people opposed to more wilderness were giving their testimony at that hearing in 1979. His old-Vermonter's credentials trump them all. Born in Woodstock in 1801, he was the grandson of the state's first Lieutenant Governor, son of a Vermont representative in Congress, and himself a member from Vermont in the U.S. House. His name is honored in many sites around the state, including the Life Sciences Building at the University of Vermont.

In 1864 Marsh published his masterpiece, *Man and Nature, or Physical Geography as Modified by Human Action.* It drew on his extensive reading and on his observations, while he was serving as United States Minister to Italy and Turkey, of dwindling agricultural productivity around the Mediterranean. Another important ingredient, however, was his memory of growing up in Woodstock at a time when Mt. Tom was denuded of trees. The erosion following such clear-cutting was so severe that mud washed through the streets of town, farms were damaged, and the contours of the mountain visibly altered. In view of such experiences, Marsh became an early and eloquent voice witnessing that human carelessness can have a palpable, destructive, and long-lasting effect upon the natural environment.

Marsh's tone in *Man and Nature* is simultaneously scientific and prophetic. As a Vermonter, he always remained especially attuned to the biological and cultural value of forests. This passage, on the wanton felling of trees, is typical of his forcefulness:

> The face of the earth is no longer a sponge, but a dust heap, and the floods which the waters of the sky pour over it hurry swiftly along its slopes, carrying in suspension vast quantities of earthy particles which increase the abrading power and mechanical force of the current . . . The washing of the soil from the mountains leaves bare ridges of sterile rock, and the rich organic mould which covered them, now swept down into the dank low grounds, promotes a luxuriance of aquatic vegetation that breeds fever, and more insidious forms of mortal disease, by its decay, and thus the earth is rendered no longer fit for the habitation of man.

Marsh argued that (with the possible exception of Oregon) no more woods should be cut down anywhere in the United States. Only by such restraint could agricultural stability and the water supply of the nation's cities be protected. His book contributed to the founding of the Adirondack Forest Preserve—in some ways the prototypical American conservation area—and of the United States Forest Service. For these reasons, according to the cultural historian Lewis Mumford, *Man and Nature* may be regarded as "the fountainhead of the conservation movement." It is a book to which we must return in tracing the wilderness ethic to its origin.

However, like Frost, Marsh also has faith in the regenerative powers of the Vermont land, and in the mutually beneficial relation between humanity and nature that comes when people can take a longer view. He too finds in the evidence of forest succession something for hope. In *Man and Nature* he writes of the need to "become a co-worker with nature . . . [and] aid her in reclothing the mountain slopes with forests and vegetable mould." The establishment of Bristol Cliffs Wilderness Area, from such a perspective, goes far beyond a chastened policy of noninterference or a taboo against humanity. It represents, rather, both our affirmation of recovered wildness and our choice to take an active role in protecting the conditions under which it flourishes. It is a decision to allow a place for wildness within culture, so that culture, in its turn, can benefit from the wildness surrounding it.

The Western wilderness ethic affirms that wilderness has integrity—that the value of land does not derive from its immediate usefulness to humans. Marsh's complementary insistence is that humanity should preserve wilderness because we too have integrity. Citizens in our region of Vermont can view ourselves not as interlopers beside the mountain brook, but as a part of the natural world, drawing strength, with the trees, from a common source. Frost is the Vermont poet in whom this dialogue is fulfilled. He sees in the losses of our state's history an opportunity for renewing our communion with nature.

Approaching the final descent to Rocky Dale, I've come to a corrugated slope that tilts down like a great staircase. This is an area of powerful winds and particularly rocky soil, so that there is always considerable blow-down between here and the river. But in the early summer shoots will take hold between the fallen logs, just as they will higher up in the landscape of fir waves. Light will pour through the broken canopy and encourage growth in these hillside intervals. For now, the snow smooths my way as I trudge downhill toward a road I'll be very glad to see again. My waffly tracks slide forward into the twilight's blank new page.

INTERVAL

Bird's-eye view of Bristol, Vermont, 1889, by George E. Norris

In the Village

➤➤➤ On my study wall, next to the old green recliner where I sit down with my journal after a hike, are two topographic maps taped together end to end. South Mountain's long elevation assumes the shape of a green finger pointing northward. Where its tip overhangs our settlement, contour lines gather and swirl into a fingerprint. Bristol has been imprinted by these heights. Reading Frost and hiking in the mountains have felt like dusting for the prints, raising the ridges of identity that plant our story here. North Mountain looms even more steeply over town, plunging down to Route 116 in the diagonal striations of the cliff called Deer Leap. On the topo map, this continuation of the Hogback Anticline, with Bristol and Monkton to its west, Starksboro and Huntington to its east, looks like another finger. The Deer Leap fingertip is pointed due south, with its tip poised just a hair's width, and a fraction to the east, away from the opposing end of Bristol Cliffs. Such geological immensities, counterposed at such a tiny gap, make it feel to someone regarding the map as if a spark should crackle through the air between them. But the opening is filled instead by a thread of blue.

The pressure and heat of converging plates smelted the Cheshire quartzite bedrock that later rose to form our anticline. It baked like an iron ingot in the belly of an antique bloomery forge. When the ridge later crumpled up to articulate the watershed, there was sometimes slippage along that steady slope of force. One such "thrust fault" opened here at the vertiginous up-down-up of Bristol Gap.

This is the ancient history we can read in the cliffs and bluffs that hang above our village, through whose topmost fringe of trees my family can watch the moon rise every evening into its dark page of stars and dreams. But no one, finally, can read the lay of the land the way a river can. The New Haven River tumbles northward out of Lincoln, the quartzite palisade of Bristol Cliffs walling it in on the western side. Howard Frank Mosher's novella refers to his north-easterly portion of Vermont as the land *Where the Rivers Flow North*. But in this part of the state, too, rivers remember the glaciers and head out after them to Canada. Two thousand meters of ice so compressed the ground that, after the glacier finally melted, there was a gradual recoil from south to north. As the rivers carved their new courses into the present interglacial period, north remained, generally speaking, the best way downhill.

Upon arriving at Bristol Gap, though, the New Haven encounters the easterly shifted face of Deer Leap, and finds that north is abruptly and steeply *up*. It's almost comical to look at this Forest Service topo map, labeled "South Mountain, Vt.," from the river's point of view. First its northward vector has to veer suddenly west, with the water's velocity maintained in its new, flatter bed by an influx from Baldwin Creek, just to the east. There are fewer huge boulders in the water after this bend, more pools harboring instead their native brook trout under a slimy snag or in the shadow of an undercut bank. After having passed through the village of Bristol, where it runs just behind Main Street, the New Haven turns sharply once more, this time to the south. It hasn't forgotten the ancestral lure of north, but is simply following the only available course through stubborn, stone-moored folds of land until it finds a confluence with the Otter Creek near the River Bend Campground in the town of New Haven. The Otter, which manages to run more consistently north along its entire course, is the principal river of western Vermont. It was an important highway for Abenaki travelers, from its arising in Rutland County until the moment when it

bestows itself into that other majestic, northward flow we know as Lake Champlain.

In the summer, when I boulder-hop along the New Haven where it curves through Bristol, I have no doubt about why the town arose just here. At Bartlett Falls, just north of our village on the Lincoln Road, stand the footings of a significant dam. There was a sawmill here early on, then a grist mill and, during the 1940s and 1950s, a hydroelectric generator. Aside from those footings, only the various spillways remain. Our family swims in the pool below the ghost-dam when July is at its hottest. Maple sometimes follows us out into the strong black water right beneath the falls, where the surface swells up round and fat like mercury. As she swims barking in circles, we dive below and tickle her feet—grateful for her ruddy, noisy life in this misty world of overhanging hemlocks, white noise, and the cold, relentless push of gravity.

I wish it were as easy to be comforted when Matthew leaps with the older boys from the gray ledges above the falls. This is a northern New England rite of passage that I, a child of California's suburbs, never experienced. All over Vermont, adolescents jump into rock-clad pools from shiny ledges high above. They egg each other on until they're leaping backward and with eyes closed, clambering higher and higher, sometimes augmenting the drop by pulling themselves out onto the highest branches of ancient white pines hanging far above the spray. Though I'm writing this particular narrative in March, I can see Matthew now, a swirl of white arms, blind to the rocks, deaf to my worries, falling through the air into the river's throat. One of the youngest of the high-dive boys, he flips his long hair back from his impassive face, emerging in teenage dignity to scale the rocks again and splash, again, into the downward swarm of water.

➤➤➤ There must be some towns that ended up where they are simply because of being halfway between two other places; or because, after the first wave of settlement, there was still some land left there; or even because, after a particularly grueling day, a tired band of pioneers decided they were never going one step farther. But there generally seems, in fact, to be a natural logic in the location of human communities on the earth, no matter how this may have been obscured by the overlying webs of trade and transportation. I once looked down at Manhattan from the roof of 500 Fifth Avenue and saw why a great city would inevitably have arisen just there, in the tremendous union of the Hudson River and the East River and the sea. To this day, multitudes of birds flow in their flyways by Manhattan's granite and marble walls, on migrations through the city that began long before the first ship came. In our smaller natural and human scale, Bristol, too, expresses the rush of water through rock, the energy of falling from the heights, the seasonal shake of life replacing life. Our village squares its houses and its streets on a little plateau tucked up against the western side of Bristol Gap, a human encampment beside the life-giving rush of the New Haven River.

This is time out from my northward hike, a respite in the village that lies between two forested leaps of land, and where my family and I lead our lives, day by day. Frost called his third volume of poetry, published in 1916, *Mountain Interval,* with "interval" referring both to a period of time spent among the mountains and to the land's division where water slices through the heights. The poet's dedication to that book's first edition read: "To you who need least reminding that before this interval of the South Branch under black mountains, there was another interval, the Upper at Plymouth, where we walked in spring beyond the covered bridge; but that the first interval of all was the old farm, our brook interval, so called by the man we had it from in sale." Human existence, personal relationships, and settlements are always encompassed by particular intervals of time and space. As I often find myself doing when I hike the mountains above Bristol and reflect about "Directive," I also remember Wordsworth's "Michael" in contemplating these topo maps in my study on North Street. It too is a poem that identifies itself with the interval opened in the heights by the rushing life of water:

> You will suppose that with an upright path
> Your feet must struggle; in such bold ascent
> The pastoral mountains front you, face to face.
> But, courage! for around that boisterous brook
> The mountains have all opened out themselves,
> And made a hidden valley of their own.

Some spaces prove suitable to harbor the life of the body and the spirit, and they are often identified by the walls surrounding them.

This gap in the cadence of my hike from South Mountain to North Mountain is like the caesura that punctuates and balances a line of verse. Such a pause offers a place to stand and heft the countervailing elements of the poetry. "Directive" as a whole has its own caesura, in line 35. After seven syntactically interwoven sentences in the first 34 lines, line 35 brings the dramatic closure of two full-stops: ". . . faded / Into each other. Both of them are lost." The poem brakes to an abrupt halt here. The sentences that follow will reinforce the sense that a new phase has now begun. First came the long enchantment of the haunted woods, the hike up past the line of being lost. Next will be the new discovery of home, as the tangled woods of history coalesce into a refreshed and livable sense of "all this now."

Unlike the California of my boyhood, where the Sierra seemed to stand majestically beyond the circle of our urban/suburban sprawl, Bristol village and the framing mountains make fullest sense when construed in terms of each other. I never understood until living in this part of New England how specific to a town like ours were the opening lines of Frost's "Stopping by Woods on a Snowy Evening."

> Whose woods these are I think I know.
> His house is in the village, though;

He will not see me stopping here
To watch his woods fill up with snow.

The woods that buffer most of the Bristol Cliffs Wilderness Area from roads are privately owned, as is North Mountain in its entirety. These ten- to fifty-acre woodlots and hunting camps are never framed by fences and rarely even marked off by the plastic tape and day-glo blazes of surveyors. Though they are private property, as landowners' rage at the Forest Service expropriations underscored, such holdings flow together in use, and in beauty, into one communal woods. They compose Bristol's forest-commons where, as long as we don't cut our neighbors' trees, we can walk and read and picnic as we like. Just as New England villagers often don't fence between their yards—thus allowing children to tumble in play along the expanse of one vast lawn dotted with their playmates' houses—so too the wooded heights of North Mountain soar above the houses like a shared inheritance.

The character of our village itself has been determined by closeness to the mountains. Though Bristol has always been both smaller and less affluent than the shiretown of Middlebury, our central village has a fuller core of contiguous streets—two and a half miles around the periphery when Rita and I take a stroll under the blazing winter stars. Furthermore, though this has never been much of a town for mansions, there are many more handsome old dwellings here than in Middlebury. Our own home, at 74 North Street, is a typical Bristol type. In it the natural, social, and economic history of our settlement may be read, just as the narrative of geology is written in the talus slopes of Bristol Cliffs.

For one thing, our house is faced with clapboards that would have been milled locally. Wood has always been in ready supply, and large houses are the rule. Our own eleven rooms, including the small addition jutting off the back that was added as some predecessor's family grew, feel like just about the standard size. Wood was cheap but slate was not, up here in the mountains. So a number of the North Street houses are also like ours in having their slates arranged in what the old-timers call "Poor Man's Roof"—a diagonal pattern that requires fewer slates than when the overlaps are parallel to a roof's edges. Our house was built in 1821. A large number of our neighbors' houses also stem from the years between 1820 and 1860, when a sawmill, a tanbark mill, a gristmill, and a box factory were humming along on the New Haven, just down the hill from the present commercial block and Holley Hall.

In 1869, a flood carried away most of the structures at the foot of what was by then called Mill Hill, and our town entered an economically depressed period during which there was little building. But by the last decade of the nineteenth century, the Bristol Manufacturing Company had established its factory by the New Haven, and had become one of the leading producers of caskets and baby carriages in the country. This cradle-to-grave concern employed one hundred and fifty people and used over a million board feet of lumber annually. The company's greatest success was from about 1895 to 1910. This was the era when our house, like so many others in the village, added a big wrap-around porch that makes it look more Victorian than its real origins. At that same time, a simple bay window was thrust out from the dining room and a more spacious interior staircase was installed. The stairs are a lovely piece of work, with elegantly turned posts in the balustrade and risers of curly maple. It also catches the eye, though, because of being crammed into a space too small for it, with the bottom banister almost touching the stair treads. It's likely that the pattern was purchased from some traveling salesman, pitching gentility and gingerbread to Vermont householders whose wallets had finally begun to thicken up a bit.

The most recent striation in the geological record of Bristol's clapboard deposition came in the 1980s. That's when many Vermonters, like Americans in general, decided that we'd rather spend than save. As I write on this frigid March day, I've moved out of the study to sit in our boxy, dark living room beside the woodstove. But when I pull my chair close to the stove's warmth, I'm looking out into the airy back of the house. We gutted the old summer kitchen and attached woodshed, installed high double windows all around and a fan window above the glass doors leading out to a new deck. Such extravagances proceeded up and down North Street, where decks, especially, have become a standard feature of the Bristol Home. We sit on ours to enjoy the warmth of summer and the colors of fall. We look through the fan window, watching the winter moon slip up above North Mountain while we eat our supper at the kitchen table.

>>> The interweaving of our life within the house and our experiences on the mountain is the biggest difference between my earlier experience of wilderness in California and my connection now with the Bristol Cliffs Wilderness Area. Then, I would go out for a couple of weeks at a time with buddies from high school or college, on expeditions to mountains much higher and more remote from settlement than any in Vermont. Everything about those outings—special bedding, special boots, special diet, detachment from the usual worlds of family, work, and school—marked them off as remote from our normal existence. They were pastoral interludes. Such wilderness camping trips reflected California's geography—both the greater distances we had to travel before camping and the higher peaks that such journeys made available. But they also followed from a tradition established by such early Sierra explorers as Clarence King and John Muir. In *Mountaineering in the Sierra Nevada* (1872) and *The Mountains of California* (1894), King and Muir, respectively, reinforced the figure of the explorer, solitary or with a male comrade, pursuing adventures far from the realm of family and culture. Their books came after the two men's returns to New York and San Francisco, as the raconteur's role succeeded that of the

mountaineer. Even as women writers have since become much more prominent in our literature of wilderness, this emphasis upon separation from the normal human community has remained common to the genre.

Our Vermont mountains are less sublime than the Sierra, but by that same token they also offer remarkable possibilities for familial integration. When I go camping in the Green Mountains, it is most likely to be with our entire family. When I go out on hikes by myself, I almost always come home at night to prepare and eat a meal with Rita and our children and to sleep in our own bed with my wife. All of us in the family take our individual outings in the nearby woods. But the shared points of reference, from Mt. Abraham to Deer Leap, are so familiar that when we share our individual stories they naturally intertwine into a collective web, like those webs of stories that also sustain Leslie Silko's Pueblo community. The nearby ledges where we have so often picnicked, and the higher ledge where Dad's ashes drifted off into a breeze two months ago, mark out the ground on which I trace my personal history as a reader and a hiker in these hills. "Directive," with its own stories of community that arise from the reorientation of a hike, helps me to frame this map of home.

The houses in our village mirror the economic and social changes in Bristol as surely as the woods that overhang our houses record the biological succession. Indeed, succession remains a notable fact in the life of our town. Most people who live in the village own their own homes, and many inherited rather than bought them. The Yankee settlers of Bristol intermarried with the French-Canadian immigrants who came at the end of the nineteenth century. Large extended families now dominate social and political life, with some, like the Bouviers, the Lathrops, and the Cousinos, having special prominence in local organizations like the Selectboard and the Fire Department. At the same time, the beautiful environment and small-town character of Bristol have attracted many newcomers, families like ours who have now seen our children through the local elementary school and into the high school, who have participated in the local churches and joined the town band or the Rescue Squad. One difference, though, is that we are not the owners of mountain woodlots left to us by our parents. Because of our own upbringing in more urban or suburban areas, we also seem more likely as a group to support zoning that will keep the surroundings of our village forested. As I write, we are anticipating a fiercely contested election for the Bristol Selectboard. Succession, here too, is the issue. Will our own children be swirled into the future leadership of Bristol, in the same way Catholic Québecois married into and transformed the Baptist and Methodist families who preceded them here? Will the Bristol Cliffs Wilderness Area, slowly subsiding into untracked forest, turn out to be the nurse-log for a new ethic of conservation and community in our mountain home?

➤➤ Here in the village, no less than in the mountains, the first and biggest story is geology. And it's not necessary to lift our eyes unto the hills to read this narrative. One of the best places to stand and recall Bristol's place on earth is right in front of Lyon's Hardware. I reach this vantage point by walking four blocks down North Street to the Green and then turning down West Street for three more blocks. Right across the road from where I stand, the land drops steeply off into a gorge filled with the buildings, and the huge piles of logs, of Lathrop's mill and lumberyard. But looking *past* the mill I also see, perhaps a mile away, the sandy lip of another bank, and a plateau exactly level with the one I'm standing on.

This is the level of an ancient delta, and it accounts for the existence of our community, here and now, on a flat, fertile tableland tucked among the hills. When the Wisconsin Glacier was beginning to melt northward, 19,000 years ago, the monolith of ice on the Champlain Valley's floor liquefied into an enormous inland sea called Lake Vermont by geologists today. Unmelted ice to the north dammed the valley's drainage, lifting the water line up to an ancient shore that ran just to the west of where Mt. Abraham High School now stands. Individual masses of ice also held on *eastward* from the lake, as if withdrawing higher up into the mountains. Streams of ice-melt from them coursed back downward through the aqueduct we now call Bristol Notch, then fanned out and let their sediment settle as their waters joined Lake Vermont. The resulting delta includes the flat land on which our own house, Lyon's Hardware, and the high school all rest. Its well-drained soil contrasts sharply with the heavy clays that resulted, just to our west, from the longer, slower, finer sedimentation farther out into the lake.

The best way to *believe* in the history of our delta-home, to let the geological idea become a gut experience, is to peer straight down at Lathrop's Mill. The New Haven River's meander, right where it bends its course from westward to southwestward in an oxbow, has carved a deep gorge, perhaps 200 feet below the level where I stand. Lathrop's buildings and sheds, scattered along the river, are dominated by two strong verticals—the large, silver-domed silo, for storing sawdust, and the round brick chimney for burning it, with LATHROP spelled out from its top to its bottom in white capitals. The gorge was long established when the lumber mill grew up there, early in the last century. Still, it seems when I look down as if the silo and chimney are being pulled into the earth by the action of the river. In fact, the agriculture and industry from which the village arose have to a significant degree already subsided into this dynamic plateau. And as surely as the hill-farms have been replaced by thick woods, our town too, sooner or later, will be folded back into the living swirl of these mountains. Such a destiny would be almost impossible to believe without this opportunity for gazing down to where the river has bared the origin and destiny of our little civic delta.

Turning to look east from the same vantage point near Lyon's, I can see right up into the origins of Bristol Notch as well. The longitudinal thrust-fault introduced a gap, and ice and water have done the rest. The top part of the notch is carved into a broad U, where the hull of a glacial schooner cut through the rippling surfaces of quartzite. Below, the opening sharpens down to a well-honed V, where, both before and after the Wisconsin Glacier's voyage, the river we now call the New Haven has been taking its own path down and in. The U topping the V in Bristol Notch recalls the U-shaped notches in the leaves of sugar maples that blanket our upper slopes, while in newer groves below them flourish red maples with their V-notched leaves. To note such analogies, in this cyclic, reiterative landscape, is to see leaves falling, rising, and unfolding forever. As Thoreau writes in "Spring," from *Walden,*

> Even ice begins with delicate crystal leaves, as if it had flowed into the moulds which the fronds of water plants have impressed on the watery mirror. The whole tree itself is but one leaf, and rivers are still vaster leaves whose pulp is intervening earth, and towns and cities are the ova of insects in their axils.

Or as Frost writes, in his poem "In Hardwood Groves": "The same leaves over and over again." And the same *ice,* revisiting Vermont in a slow earth-flicker over the past two million years, glaciers disappearing through their U-shaped notches back up into the heights. And now I too am ready to retreat again, up onto the Hogback spine of North Mountain, and to walk north until I reach the water, and "Directive"'s end.

NORTH MOUNTAIN

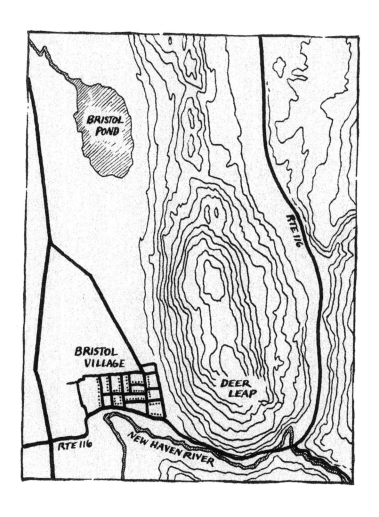

North Mountain Gyres

And if you're lost enough to find yourself
By now, pull in your ladder road behind you
And put a sign up CLOSED to all but me.
Then make yourself at home . . .

⧉ With these four lines that move from "lost" to "home," a new stage commences in "Directive." The original impulse for hiking up into the poem's heights was retreat, and the first result was disorientation amid the haunted woods. But disorientation still relates to one's former—even if no longer available—bearings. At a certain point, one stops looking backward anxiously over one's shoulder and settles in to make the most of a new situation. The direction to "pull in your ladder road behind you / And put a sign up CLOSED to all but me" signals an end to the steep ascent, and a severing of past associations and relationships. Let the dead bury the dead.

This is also a new phase of my own passage up the rocky spine that backs Bristol. I've crossed the New Haven River now, and I'm on the northern side where the village and our family's house lie. The next several hikes I take will thus be within sight of our home, and of the schools our children attend. My footsteps will traverse private property, whereas up until now they have led largely through federally protected wilderness. This crossing reflects a larger transition in our family's orientation to the woods. For a long time, as Rita and I have raised our three children in rural New England, we figured that we might well gravitate back to northern California at some point. We were merely sojourners—resident, and possibly temporary, Out-of-Staters. Over the past several years, though, we have realized that this place might be where we were actually going to live—where we had in fact been living all along, in this cut-over, small-scale, intricately interwoven terrain. In our family life and in our environmental values, too, it was time, and past time, to pull up the ladder road and make ourselves at home.

Deer Leap is the dominant feature in the topography beside our home. When we swim in the pool below Bartlett Falls, its crags soar above, filling the northern sky with their pronounced striations that angle sharply downward from east to west. The enormous earth-powers that can thrust up and displace huge plates of rock disclose themselves here, right before our eyes. On our long summer afternoons in the river, the Deer Leap rocks gather warmth and color over our heads until the cliff diffracts into a spectrum of browns, reds, and ochers.

Looking up from the falls like this, one has the most dramatic view of this face. But when hiking to the top of it I follow a route that leads directly up from our back-porch door, on the western side of Deer Leap. With Maple on a leash, to make sure she behaves herself, I head up Fitch Avenue past the Rescue Squad garage where Rita spent so much time during her years as an EMT. At the top of the block lives the long-haired Lab-mix dog who is Maple's bitter enemy. No words of mine could stop our otherwise mild pet from hurling herself snarling on this monster of iniquity, so I pull the leash snug and quickly turn right on Mountain Street. She and I both relax as we pass the Bristol Elementary School, a sprawling brick complex that Rachel, Matthew, and Caleb all attended. The larger wing of the school is an addition voted in a few years back, right before the taxpayers in our county got so cranky. It includes a copper roof and a gymnasium, along with nice little touches like marble lintels over the doors and windows and a beautifully carved and painted wooden sign. Behind the school is an enormous field where, whether the season has brought them mud, grass, fallen leaves, or snow, flocks of school kids wheel and screech through their long-awaited recesses.

About a block past the school comes another turn, left onto Mountain Terrace, the last cul-de-sac before the trees reassert their old prerogatives. I let Maple off the leash now and roll it up in the knapsack. She races the length of Mountain Terrace and enters the woods on a dirt road that I reach myself five minutes later. There's a padlocked chain across the entrance of this road, which is used only by the Bristol Water Department truck for periodic checks of the town reservoir. I sit on that arc of chain to tighten my bootlaces, making sure my coattails come between me and its steel on this chilly morning. As far as the sky is concerned (if not the air), spring has arrived. Days are already much longer and there's a golden quality to the light. Chickadees and nuthatches, for whom light is the main seasonal marker, have been purposefully in evidence on my recent hikes, though still puffed up almost round against the wind's edge. And it's about time to see the first robins in our yard.

Maple intermittently barrels back down the trail toward me, snorting little clouds of steam in her excitement. To my right lie the steeply tilted back-acres of the houses on East Street, while to the left are woods that have been fairly heavily logged in recent decades. But some large handsome beeches remain close to the trail, and at the first little plateau, where there is a dogleg to the left, rises a magnificent white pine beneath which our family used to picnic when the children were small. It towers so high that the fantasy always flits through my mind to search in the bark for one of the carved arrow-marks that would have designated it as a Royal Pine, reserved for use as a mast in the British Navy of the Georges' time. But, as always, I keep walking. Another turn to the right, one more to the left, and the next plateau appears, occupied by the cyclone-fenced town reservoir.

Immediately, the truck-width dirt road comes to an end, succeeded by a hiking trail that rises eastward and then turns almost due north through much thicker growth. Boulders constantly break through the soil, and paper birches cluster along the trail's western side. On an early spring day like this, peach-pink tones glow with special warmth through the peeling flaps of their powdery white bark. I never knew the best way to reach Deer Leap from this village side, and spent years casting around ineffectually in the intervening terrain of gullies and outcrops. But just last month Louise Brynn, who grew up here, gave me the right bearings. She said to look for an especially prominent boulder at the left side of the trail, then turn perpendicularly onto an old logging road that would lead off to the right. At first this track is obscure, but then it becomes quite obvious for almost all of the way to Deer Leap.

The logging road finally dead-ends at an explosion of crumpled rock that Maple, even with all her grand enthusiasm, could not conceivably traverse. This is where we head north again, to circle around the brow of Deer Leap from the gradually rising land to that side. We will not climb to the top of the cliff in this season, lest we bother the peregrine falcons who lay their eggs on the crumbly ledge just below the drop-off. Instead, we'll find our own perch decisively below that height and to the southeast of it. Above us as we walk wheel three turkey vultures, each pair of wings raised in a V, and with light shining through their long primary feathers. But I'm also hoping today to see the stupendous dive of a falcon, folding the air between the rocky summit and the forest cover hundreds of feet below. The return of peregrines to Bristol represents new possibilities for harmony between the human and nonhuman citizens here, in our chosen place on earth.

> Turning and turning in the widening gyre
> The falcon cannot hear the falconer;
> Things fall apart; the centre cannot hold . . .

With the image of a departing falcon, Yeats's "The Second Coming" represents the chaos at an era's end. Instead of focusing obediently on the falconer, the bird swings farther and farther away, then abandons contact altogether. Its disappearance signals the insecurity when one chapter of history draws to a close, with no one certain what the next age will be like. But Yeats, like Frost, welcomed the reinvigoration of the new, whatever uncertainties attended it.

In August, after our peregrines have safely raised another clutch of chicks without human interference, I will return to look down from the top of Deer Leap at fledglings lingering near the aerie of their origin. I always like remembering Yeats's term "gyre" when I watch falcons wheeling above this ridge of the Green Mountains near our Bristol home. It's a sharply angled word, conveying the tilts and accelerations within their circling flight. A slow, floating curve can suddenly warp downward at Mach speed when a falcon glimpses prey, or when it simply wants to revel in being the swiftest, most acrobatic diver our earth's skies have ever known.

Vermonters are watching falcons' flight with special interest now because, after thirty years in which our mountains never saw them stoop on a jay or heard their high-pitched *kek-kek-kek,* a vast, eccentric gyre has finally carried them back. If they continue returning each spring to their reestablished nests in our state, it will confirm that they have really circled home; something that fell apart will have been set right.

Peregrines had disappeared from every state east of the Mississippi by 1960. DDT, concentrated in the food chain as it moved link by link toward these magnificent predators, diminished their ability to metabolize calcium and made their eggs too thin to incubate and hatch. Rachel Carson's *Silent Spring,* first serialized in the *New Yorker* and then appearing as a book in 1962, called America's attention to the devastation of insect and bird life caused by the pesticide. Because of her writing, congressional hearings were held that resulted in banning the use of DDT within the United States. However, since there were by that time no breeding pairs of peregrines left in New England, the population could only begin to recover in our region through the concerted efforts of human beings.

The word "recover" is not quite right. The original subspecies of the Northeast, *Falco peregrinus anatum Bonaparte,* is now extinct. The falcons reintroduced here have thus been a mixed group of North American and European subspecies, the theory being that natural selection will determine which of these closely related varieties is best suited to our environment. The reintroduction, supported by a cooperative effort at Cornell University involving the Peregrine Fund and the United States Fish and Wildlife Service, made use of a technique first employed by falconers in medieval Europe. Chicks hatched in captivity were "hacked"—placed in a nesting box and provided with food while they learned to hunt on their own. Medieval falconers regularly recaptured the birds, so that they would also learn to return to human masters with their prey. But the new hackers kept scrupulously out of contact with the falcon chicks, wanting to see them gain independence from humans. During a five-year period starting in 1982, when hacking sites were being operated in Vermont, over one hundred peregrines were released. To put this figure in perspective, experts believe that there were probably never more than four hundred breeding pairs east of the Mississippi. The hackers' efforts, though by no means always successful, thus made a significant start toward restoring the peregrines to their original number.

I find this process of reintroduction significant and moving, and also a little funny. It expresses a less human-centered perspective on the physical creation, as well as showing how up-to-date scientific knowledge may be applied in a careful, effective act of restitution. The peregrine project's success is all the more remarkable when one remembers how these birds, like other animals that prey on creatures we might prefer to eat ourselves, were reviled in the last century. They were called duck hawks, big-footed hawks, or simply vermin, and people did what they could (which was relatively little before DDT, given the inaccessibility of their nest sites) to exterminate them. But we are now calling the peregrines by a nobler title and going to great lengths to save them. As they return to Vermont from their long circle through extinction, they show how far we too have come. The name "peregrine" itself, from the Latin for traveler, and with its English connotation of pilgrim, also captures the purposeful aspect of our own human journey. In devoting such effort to building up a population of birds destroyed by our heedlessness, we are also exploring environmental values higher than monetary profit or utility.

My excitement in today's hike to the top of Deer Leap is enhanced because this is one of the reestablished sites where peregrines annually build their nests. I like to come up here so that I can remember to look at Bristol from their perspective. When the hacking began in Vermont, this was one of a number of places researchers kept their eyes on. It had all the requisites for an aerie: a steep cliff, facing south so that it would receive the sun and generate the rising columns of warm air called thermals; a rock face rugged enough to hold niches for nesting and to be isolated from most human activity; and a good supply of prey, including the jays, grouse, tanagers, flickers, and robins living along the woodland-and-meadow edge beneath the cliff's foot and the pigeons venturing out from several nearby barns.

Sure enough, in 1986 a pair of peregrines scouted our cliffs. But they were apparently discouraged by logging near the base. In 1987 they or a different pair established their nest on a westward-angled ledge, only to abandon that site, possibly because of human interference. That same season they returned, though, and staked out a more protected aerie on the eastward face. They successfully hatched clutches of eggs there in both 1987 and 1988. Then, in 1989, they switched over to a nearby raven's nest that had been abandoned. The Bristol peregrines have generally had better luck with their fledglings

than the average Vermont survival rate of 50 percent. In 1988 three chicks got fairly far along before two of them suddenly disappeared, most likely snatched by a great horned owl. But in 1989 all three of the new chicks made it to the phase of hardy juveniles, and since 1990 we've generally enjoyed two or three fully fledged chicks a year. Once peregrines have really found their wings, they have no reason to fear any other avian predator.

I was first taken up to see the peregrines by Randy Durand, a Bristol high school science teacher who monitors the aerie on a volunteer basis for the Vermont Institute of Natural Science. He also was responsible, after the 1987 pair were driven away on their first approach, for posting large red signs on tree trunks along that section of the ridge:

Peregrine Falcon Nesting Area
Please Do Not Trespass Beyond
the Posted Area.
(Mar. 1–Aug. 1)
Why? Peregrine falcons will
abandon their nest ledges if
humans climb to a nearby
equivalent level or climb to a
point ABOVE their nest ledge.

For what Time Period? During
the Courtship (March–April), Incubation (April–May),
Hatching (May–June), and Fledging
(June–July) stages.

When he took me up it was fall, past the danger point for disrupting their fledging period, so we hiked all the way to the top of the cliff. Along the way, though, he showed me the lookout where Maple and I have come today. Since this ledge for watching the peregrines in spring is both lower and smaller than the crown of Deer Leap, Randy has named it Fawn Leap. From here, with the aid of binoculars, I can see right across the rocky amphitheater to the nest. It is the perfect vantage point for observing the peregrines without disturbing them.

As Maple and I bushwhacked to this spot, we passed several enormous white oaks, remnants of the stands that grew in our area before the nineteenth century. They were cut for the local coffin works, as well as for making shoe lasts. The land we have been walking through is all private, a patchwork of small parcels. But because of its rugged terrain it forms a sort of accidental nature preserve, even richer in natural variety than the Bristol Cliffs Wilderness rising on the other side of Route 116. The pink lady's slipper, or moccasin flower, grows throughout, along with stands of the lady's slipper's rarer yellow form. Many deer shelter in these steep coves, and moose occasionally wander through. In addition there are black bear, coyotes, red foxes, and—according to more than one witness—a panther.

Vermont's six official wilderness areas are focal points for the process of natural reclamation. But there are also many areas like Bristol's North Mountain—privately held, multiple-use lands enriching the lives of people in the nearby towns. Deer Leap, with its peregrine-encircled cliffs, looms right above our village. This spectacular upland forms a seasonally changing backdrop for children playing in the field behind Mountain Street school. Walking down North Street to go shopping, visit the post office, or attend one of the three churches in the village, residents of our town are accompanied by the mountain. And when we are driving home from Burlington on the Monkton Road, the ridge slowly rising to our east shows that now we're getting close. Our town's most prominent feature is nothing we have built. The mountain itself was the first and most important landholder in Bristol.

Loggers work away in the flatter acreage around North Mountain's skirts. Coming up toward the reservoir in spring and fall, I always find the tread marks of their trucks pressed deeply into the wet soil, just as a mile or so further up the slopes I sometimes have come upon the tracks of black bears. Loggers and bears; blueberries, deer-hunters, and falcons—these define the true "multiple use" that has been sanctioned, and sanctified, by North Mountain. Like many lit-tle towns in northern New England and upstate New York, Bristol is struggling now to plan for its future as a vital community. But when it comes to issues of zoning, polarization can occur quickly, and tempers run high. Perhaps this topic is even hotter here than in some neighboring towns because of the living memories, and emo-tions, from the Bristol Cliffs controversy.

But when I listen in Howden Hall, our community center, to a debate about adopting a town plan, it seems to me that people on both sides are all essentially calling for preservation of the status quo. The difference is that for some this means preventing develop-ment that will subdivide our mountains or blur the focus of our central village, while for others it means upholding the rights of landowners to do what they want with their own property. But the true situation seems to me that Vermont has already experienced enormous *change* throughout the last century and a half. After the abandonment of the hill-farms and the disappearance of the sheep industry, our towns have gradually become surrounded by de facto wilderness—making them fresher, more beautiful, and more free. We'll only be able to reach wise decisions about our collective fu-ture if we begin by acknowledging the transformations that have brought about this balance of settled and wooded lands, with its remarkable possibilities for an integrated life in nature.

The return of our forests was nothing that anyone planned. When the flinty hill-farms were abandoned, a natural progression turned fields into sumac tangles, which gave way in their turn to dense woods. On the other hand, the peregrine falcons would never be in Vermont today were it not for human work to bring them back. The falcon's return sharpens the edge of a wilderness that is new. Detoxifying the landscape and escorting peregrines into these mountains may also promise our own return from the impoverishments of prodigality. The peregrines may signal a new stage in our cultural evolution, in which we can recognize and value the diverse community of life embracing our towns.

⧽⧽⧽ One of the first things I noticed when our family settled in Vermont twenty-two years ago was the surprising absence of fences, both in the villages and in the woods. If I spent a few hours of study in the Town Clerk's office and then took to the hills with a topo map and compass I could probably identify North Mountain's 10- and 20-acre parcels as I hiked, and most landowners do have a good idea which trees they can cut and which ones their neighbors get. But for hunters in the fall, snowshoers in the winter, and wildflower fanciers in the spring, these hills are the town's playground and commons.

Tramping around this stretch of the Green Mountains, especially when passing stone walls or cellar holes, I realize that the slopes feel much more communal now than would have been the case early in the last century when they were covered with working farms. They have reverted to woods and wildness as the fences have gradually tumbled down, making available as a commons land that, in legal terms, remains divided into discrete pieces of private property. Failure, like success, may take root in the land. Perhaps the fragments of a life, like instable molecules, offer better opportunities for sympathetic connection than a fulfilled and final history would.

Once more, "Michael" enhances my understanding of "Directive" and Vermont. Michael and Luke, father and son, were to have built a stone sheepfold together, symbolizing both their bond with the land and their personal unity. When Luke failed to return to his home, his aged father continued working on what was to be their shared project, but he "left the work unfinished when he died." The poem concludes

> and the remains
> Of the unfinished Sheep-fold may be seen
> Beside the boisterous brook of Green-head Ghyll.

From the perspective of Michael and his neighbors, this tale is one of failure—the loss of a family bond and the disappearance of a pastoral way of life. But Wordsworth finds in the shattered circle of the sheepfold an invitation, for connection with a family whose story would have been far less accessible if the circle were complete. Strangers would not necessarily have been welcome to a functioning farm whose livestock were safely sheltered within an intact sheepfold, any more than Frost's farm family, as imagined in "Directive," would have expected hikers in the fields beside their house. But a pile of stones amid the hills is like a doorway to connection, both with the vanished farmers whose means of livelihood is long gone and with the possibility of a continuing human and natural community. "Directive" and "Michael" both celebrate the vividness of past efforts in their landscapes and offer the possibility of sympathetic renewal for those entering the poems' carefully plotted topographies. As Wordsworth wrote in framing his tale of Michael's family,

> Therefore, although it be a history
> Homely and rude, I will relate the same
> For the delight of a few natural hearts;
> And, with yet fonder feeling, for the sake
> Of youthful Poets, who among these hills
> Will be my second self when I am gone.

Wordsworth and Frost encourage a form of sympathy that enters into the history of our predecessors in the land, and that appropriates their property and projects, in an emotional sense, at least. Roaming the woods and hills is a physical form of identification with the unfolding, collective life of our home on earth. Thus, though I neither hunt nor snowmobile, I have come to feel sympathetic with longtime residents of my town who do when they complain about the fencing and posting of acreage by new landowners. When he wrote his essay "Walking," Thoreau looked around at his part of New England and lamented the pace of privatization and enclosure. He feared the day when his landscape would be

> partitioned off into so-called pleasure-grounds, in which a few will take a narrow and exclusive pleasure only,—when fences shall be multiplied, and man-traps and other engines invented to confine men to the public road, and walking over the surface of God's earth shall be construed to mean trespassing on some gentleman's grounds. To enjoy a thing exclusively is commonly to exclude yourself from the true enjoyment of it. Let us improve our opportunities, then, before the evil days come.

Thoreau longed for a different attitude toward the land, for "a people who would begin by burning the fences and let the forests stand!" George Perkins Marsh echoed Thoreau in 1864, calling upon each of his fellow citizens to "become a co-worker with nature in the reconstruction of the damaged fabric which the negligence or the wantonness of the former lodgers has rendered untenantable." Vermont today looks as if we had in fact taken the advice of these two ancestors in the land, although the reality is that our state's being far more heavily forested today than when Marsh was growing up in Woodstock is more an accident of history than a human accomplishment. Still, in important ways the cultural climate here has greened along with the hills. The trees came back on their own, but the peregrines required our help.

➤➤ In Bristol, we have a favorite sledding slope called Devino Hill—right in the village, behind the offices and storage depot for Jackman's Fuels. On a sunny weekend with good snow cover, one is always sure to find a couple of dozen people there—mostly kids, but with a scattering of parents stamping our numb feet like waiting horses. In addition to the old-fashioned sleds with metal runners, there's also invariably a flotilla of plastic saucers, inflatable snow tubes, and snowboards. On a Sunday afternoon in February, our younger son Caleb and I went over to Devino's so that he could try out his new snow tube. (We left the dog home so she wouldn't race behind him barking and trying to pull off his hat.) I stood at the top of the hill, next to a charred circle where someone had made a bonfire the night before to enjoy the full moon over the snow, and watched Caleb steering for the jump that would send him airborne. Standing next to me, at a breather in their own sledding, a boy and girl were talking about how many people were there. She said that her father wanted to buy Devino Hill so that he could keep it from being so crowded when they wanted to go sledding. "How about all the kids who like to come here?" the boy asked. She replied, "Don't worry, my dad says we'll make a list of people who can sled and you'll be on it." But he was still not satisfied. "What about everybody else?"

I wanted to cheer (but didn't) as the boy defended his community's right to keep on enjoying the hill, no matter who owned it. In the same sense, North Mountain with its peregrines belongs to all of us, as we in turn belong to it. This is not a legal fact but, rather, a grounded myth—a story that tells us where we have come from and where our life derives its meaning. The nineteenth-century farmers and sheepherders who abandoned the woods around Deer Leap no more sought to restore their lands to thick forest than the modern farmers who employed DDT as an insecticide intended to kill the falcons. In each case, their actions had unsuspected results. But there do come certain moments in the history of a community when people can look around and say, "Well, here we are. What's next?" We have arrived at such a pause for clarification and decision in Vermont. Our providential wilderness cannot be taken for granted today. Because for a century we stood outside America's economic mainstream, our region's nonhuman community enjoyed a rare opportunity to recover. But in this new era of telecommunications, when business is no longer so closely tied to major manufacturing centers, there will be no more security for beautiful backwaters. Unless we find the will to protect the North Mountains of our state—as terrain in which selective logging, human recreation, and wildlife can coexist—we could lose within just a few seasons the balance that has grown up here. These are the real issues that spiral around our Howden Hall discussions about whether or not to institute a town master plan. North Mountain with its peregrines is a surprising gift which we can gratefully choose to accept. If we compare what it means to the life of Bristol with what selling their ridges for second homes has meant to towns on the other side of the Green Mountains, we should find little difficulty in saying where our community's true freedom lies.

Decades before eastern peregrines were driven into extinction by DDT, Louis Agassiz Fuertes, the American painter of birds, produced a beautiful watercolor of a falcon perching on a rocky ledge with its prey, a male green-winged teal. The mature female peregrine hunches fiercely over her limp victim, the rich bluish-gray of the raptor's wing and tail feathers set off by the yellow that rings her eye as well as colors her claw and the base of her curved beak. Fuertes carefully depicts details such as the notch in her beak that enables the falcon to sever the prey's spinal cord with one quick nip. The teal's reddish head hangs backward off the ledge, while the dove-gray plumage of his wing and tail, with its striking black and white bars, is propped up on display by the claw with which the predator guards her kill. The breast plumage of the two birds is the same gray-flecked, creamy tone.

The Arm and Hammer Company had commissioned Fuertes to make two series of paintings showing songbirds and birds of passage. These were reproduced on cards and enclosed in their boxes of baking soda as popular items for collectors. But when Fuertes did another series on birds of prey, the company rejected them out of a fear that such images of ferocity and killing would offend its customers. Today, predators like the gray wolf and the peregrine have become much more widely appreciated. Many find in their beauty the essence of wildness, and realize that the honed economy of the falcon's form and flight reflects her hunter's function in the food chain. Peregrine and teal, wing to wing on that windy outcropping, have co-evolved, spiraling together through the sky. Predation is a circle, not a line. The sharp curve of the peregrine's beak and the teal's flat black bill both tell the story of this woodland where beeches hold their papery, tan leaves throughout the winter, of this landscape where cliffs crumpled up to form the Green Mountains when the Adirondack coasts collided with the encroaching offshore plate. In the moment Fuertes captured, the teal is about to become a peregrine, the peregrine a teal. Can our towns too now find themselves in the surrounding woods, and bring the providential wilderness home?

The Ledges

BRISTOL LEDGES
APRIL 27, 1995

> The only field
> Now left's no bigger than a harness gall.
> First there's the children's house of make-believe,
> Some shattered dishes underneath a pine,
> The playthings in the playhouse of the children.
> Weep for what little things could make them glad.
> Then for the house that is no more a house,
> But only a belilaced cellar hole,
> Now slowly closing like a dent in dough.
> This was no playhouse but a house in earnest.

Rita and I walked up to the Bristol Ledges after supper last night for an impromptu camp-out. Our three kids were present and accounted for at home, and promised to take care of each other until we returned in time for breakfast in the morning. It was to be a full moon and the evening, if not exactly warm, was our mildest yet this spring season. We both wore our backpacks, though they were lightly loaded—mine with just the tent, our pads, and pillows, hers with our sleeping bags, water bottles, and a thermos of coffee. Though we often came up to this beautiful spot overlooking our home in the village, the present outing was Rita's idea. I was registering the still air and clear light of this late April evening with a grudging mind, having put off my return to the mountains, and to this project of reading and writing, since our golden retriever Maple had died a couple of weeks before.

Maple had been my companion among the heights for the past nine years. I'd always felt exhilarated by her bursts of enthusiasm up and down the trail, and laughed at her look of crazed excitement as she flung herself nose first into the underbrush. But this winter she had begun experiencing seizures, controllable with phenobarbital, but only at the cost of dopiness and a heartbreaking loss of vitality. In the days before her death she lay in our local animal hospital, unable to stand and finally, it seemed, blind. A specialist we consulted in Williston said that she had a tumor in her right frontal lobe. Such tumors grow inside rather than on the surface of a dog's brain, she said, so that surgery held small promise. I requested that Maple be put to sleep, lingered with her cooling body in the antiseptic examining room with its gleaming steel table, and finally left her there for cremation. The seasons since my father's death in August had felt like a war of attrition. First came my mother's ups and downs following surgery. Then Matthew had withdrawn sullenly from us, as if he were a hostage from some enemy tribe. And now, so suddenly, we had lost our sweet old hiking companion. I was stunned by all of these worries and separations, and Rita took the lead to get us out under a sky where something new was happening.

➤➤ Though it always requires some care to find Deer Leap, working eastward from the reservoir, the Ledges themselves are impossible to miss. Having turned northward after the reservoir road subsides to a trail, we just continued along a well beaten path that skirts the western edge of a bouldery plateau. The wet black ground held crisp prints from the boots of all the townsfolk who had preceded us here over the past several days. This is the best used trail in Bristol, in every season of the year. In the summer, high-schoolers come up to the Ledges for Friday night parties. We have often seen their bonfires, pulsing orange planets that hang high above our backyard, when we have stepped out after dinner to see the stars and give Maple a final airing. Just about half a mile after that large, riven boulder where I turn toward the right when paying a visit to the peregrines, the Ledges open out immediately to the left of the trail.

This is a short hike, one that never offers the fruitful confusion of getting lost amid the ancient relics of the heights. But it still has a special richness because of the countless times our family, in every permutation and combination, has come up here over the past sixteen years. The Ledges consist of a beautiful terrace of quartzite, sloping down over a western vista that includes the entire village of Bristol as well as the distant Adirondacks and Lake Champlain. The village itself is laid out almost perfectly by the points of the compass. North Street bounds the main grid, as the principal street closest to North Mountain. Rita and I settled down to drink a cup of coffee and enjoy the view before putting up our tent, noting with relief that our house was still standing in its place, right below us and a little to the right. The sky's last golden light gleamed on its slate roof, and there was neither a fire truck nor an ambulance in the driveway.

Off to the north of our house is the Mountain Street School, with its flat black roofs and large playing fields. Those fields are the biggest open space right in the village, which is bounded by two east-west streets that intersect with North Street. Pine Street, dead-ending into our yard just past the house, runs for a couple of blocks past clapboard houses like ours, then past trailers that mark a transition to the nonresidential part of town. On the left, after them, come larger industrial buildings where Autumn Harp manufactures non-petroleum-based lip balms and cosmetics. And just beyond them are the municipal buildings where the town trucks are kept, as well as the bins where we all meet on Saturday morning to sort our recycling, and the dump with its seagull-choired drifts of garbage, its neighborhoods of dead refrigerators, its mountains of composting leaves, and, at this season, its browning Christmas trees.

Main Street bounds Bristol village to the south and completes the main grid. Our one traffic light stands on the corner of Main and North, where the Bavarian-looking clock tower of Holley Hall looms across from the Green. Merchants Bank, the Post Office, and Park Texaco are Holley Hall's neighbors to the west. Across the street to the east run the commercial establishments of town—Bristol Insurance, Bristol Publishing, Cubber's Pizza, Bristol Bakery, the State Liquor Store, Bristol Paint and Glass, Deer Leap Books. Many of the buildings in this block have flat roofs and oversize facades that make Main Street look more like the downtown of a little Western town than like a Vermont village. Even after supper on a weekday, this little business strip has a steady stream of cars cruising along like big fish in a small aquarium. Sitting here, we can catch the rhythmic winking of the sunset through their curved windshields.

The grid trails off more gradually on the west than on the other three sides. The dump in effect marks the northwest corner, while Mt. Abraham High School is the main feature on our southwest boundary. Like the elementary school, it is surrounded by playing fields. But it's also distinguished by a large parking lot, and its flat roofs are covered with white gravel, not with black asphalt. Mt. Abraham is a union school, serving the towns of Lincoln, New Haven, Monkton, and Starksboro as well as Bristol. The corner of Vermont most distinguished from the rest of the state by its wildness and old-fashioned towns is known as the Northeast Kingdom. This northeastern corner of Addison County, too, has its own character. There are farms up here, but they are separately grafted among the ridges rather than expansively rolling down to the lake like the ones in Cornwall and Shoreham to our west. Forestry, gravel extraction, hunting, and cabins in the woods all contribute to the character of our district. It has traditionally been a pretty rough place, too, with more than its share of proud, cantankerous individualists. Bristol, because of its several lumberyards and its Grand Union and Brooks standing where the old Bristol Inn used to be, and because it is home to Mt. Abe High School, two banks, and several churches, is the region's unofficial capital.

➤➤➤ When Rita and I moved here with Rachel, then a two-year-old, in the summer of 1979, we had a couple of experiences that agreed with the frontier-town look of Main Street and that heightened the contrast between this more brawling, precarious town and the relatively sedate shiretown of Middlebury. At that time, one of Bristol's landmarks was an elegant little restaurant on Main Street called Mary's (which has since moved a few miles out of town to become a bed and breakfast). After one of our first weeks of steaming off moldering wallpaper, having floors refinished, patching plaster, and otherwise settling in, we were taken out to dinner at Mary's by Mark Festa, a friend and former Middlebury student whose own home was in Springfield, Massachusetts.

Rita, Rachel, Mark, and I were sitting at a round table in Mary's little bow window, our space defined by the candles and the wine glasses beside our plates, when all of a sudden there was a tremendous racket from just about five feet away. Cars on Main Street are parked facing into the curb. Immediately across from our window was the long hood of a faded green Pontiac, and one young man had thrown another one up on this hood the better to pound on him. The din was terrific, as if someone were wailing away on a large piece of sheet metal with a hammer, and we could see very clearly the aggressor's rising and falling fist. With the clove-and-cinnamon aroma of our pumpkin soup rising around our faces and the bases of our wine glasses nestled in our hands, we experienced a severe case of cognitive dissonance while hearing and witnessing that beating so close by. But while we sat there stupefied, a woman from a nearby table bolted out the door and began yelling "Stop that! Leave him alone!" The spell was broken, and the rest of us near the front door of Mary's rushed after her to lend moral support. The conqueror, a skinny kid in jeans and a tee shirt, looked around at us as if he too had been startled from a dream, jerked his victim up by his own tee shirt, and hustled him down the alley beside Mary's, beating him at intervals as they scuffed off in the direction of the New Haven River, one block away. Along with the restaurant's other patrons, our little party watched them leave, looked at the blank, undented hood, and trickled back to our meals without further comment. Did this just happen? What next?

Within that same week came another event reinforcing our sense that, in moving twelve miles northeast of Middlebury, we had somehow come to the Wild West. Rachel was asleep upstairs and Rita and I were scraping more wallpaper off the dining room walls with the help of a steamer and wide putty knives. This room, too, like the one where we'd been sitting at Mary's, has a bay window. Through the glass we could hear the F-16 whine of a truck and a motorcycle racing each other up North Street toward our house at top speed. The motorcycle was on the right side of the road, while the truck was revving along beside him in the left lane with an exuberant youth firing a shotgun into the air as he stood in the truck's bed. This really happened. Perhaps it was the gunfire, or perhaps the truck made a companionable swerve. At any rate, half a block before the contestants pulled even with our house, the motorcyclist lost control and flew out over his bike. Hurtling along as if auditioning for a job as the Human Cannonball, he collided head-on with a section of telephone pole that marked the division between our driveway and our neighbor's. His helmet split right down the middle and he lay, felled, across our yard as we and our neighbors waited for the police and rescue squad to arrive. Rita and I telephoned the hospital the next day to see what happened to the cyclist, expecting that death or paralysis were the only alternatives. But he was, apparently, fine except for a few scrapes and a speeding ticket.

A vibration had been set up for us, though, by these glimpses of violence in our new hometown. Driving home from Middlebury each afternoon as the college year started, I'd pass the young guys sitting in their cars by the Green or smoking in the bandstand. They'd stare at all the passersby, looking, I felt, for trouble. When Halloween approached, we learned that Bristol staged the most ambitious program in the county on October 30th. Cabbage Night, the traditional date for pranks, had gotten more and more out of hand. A few years back, some of the boys from the Green had started jumping on the hood and roof of a car that stopped at Bristol's solitary traffic light one Cabbage Night. I never heard whether or not they knew the driver. Regardless, he was not amused. The result was show-stopping violence on the street right in front of Holley Hall.

In this new era, between dances for the big kids and a parade for the younger ones, Cabbage Night and Halloween went off without a hitch. But just as Rita and I were beginning to relax with colder weather and a respite from what had seemed a dangerous summer and fall, a final event sharpened the edgy feeling of our new home. We'd gone to bed at the end of a long day in early November. In my dream I heard a loud pounding, like the fight in front of Mary's, but I was so disoriented it took a while before I realized where it was coming from. Someone was standing on our front porch, beating on the door as loudly as he could with his fists. I finally shook myself awake, pulled on a robe, and ran downstairs to open the door. As I looked across North Street, though, I saw that he had by now run to our neighbor on the corner of Pine and, after having knocked frantically there, was just being admitted. We had not met that neighbor, an elderly woman who moved away shortly thereafter. To this day, I have no idea who the pounder in the darkness was, what he needed, what call I did not answer. A little too sleepy, and perhaps a little scared as well, I came to the door only in time to see him run away as wildly as he'd come.

➤➤ Before it got too dark, Rita and I set up our little dome tent on a relatively flat place tucked between two red oaks and on some cushioning soil between the Ledges and the trail. We'd been thinking about those early, wild impressions of Bristol in part because Matthew at fourteen seemed to be turning into a local tough-guy in training. He was smoking, coughing, spitting, and perfecting his drop-dead stare. We sometimes felt in our own home as if we were clueless middle-aged drivers cruising back and forth beside the village Green with its contemptuous adolescent gallery. But now, having contemplated the grid of streets that mapped our present and our past alike, we spread out the bags and got ready for nightfall.

The sky was clear, and the moon was already rising behind us. There seemed absolutely no chance of rain, so we didn't bother putting the fly on the tent. We did zip up the screen door to keep out a rising choir of mosquitoes and gnats, but with the tent's opened flap and its mesh top it was still about as bright inside as out. We watched as the village and the high school were outlined by emerging strands of light. Over the next hour, those street lamps seemed to dim again as the moon slid overhead and into view. First, it bathed us in light from behind the tent, then it cast black shadows from the oak trees down over our bags, and finally it blazed right in the door so that we could see each other's faces with perfect clarity. A wind arose with the moon. We lay as if drugged under that sky that was brilliantly moonlit until after 3:00 A.M., in a tent whose sides billowed in and out with the night's slow pulse.

Eventually, when we had stopped talking and lay quietly in our warm bags, my own thoughts ran to another event associated with the Ledges. It was a forest fire in the summer of 1982 that changed my perspective on the tough boys who hang around the Green. I always think of it when I hike up to the Ledges, since it was a fire that found its epicenter in this rock. Because of our rainy climate and moist soil, as well as the general dampness of decaying matter that carpets these woodlands, the mountains of Vermont are sometimes called the asbestos forest. In contrast to the woods west of the 100th meridian, where, as Smokey warns, one match can start a forest fire, it's next to impossible to get a respectable conflagration started out here. But in late July of that year, one did kindle, right below the Ledges.

In the morning a column of light gray smoke was rising from the ridge, and by afternoon it had thickened into a dark gray cloud. By 5:00 P.M. it was looking quite serious, with the orange of flames snapping through the smoke. Men returning home from work began walking up the reservoir trail with shovels and axes over their shoulders to settle this blaze right next to our village. Arriving at the Ledges with my own garden spade, I joined a line of men that reminded me of the dwarfs on their way home from the mines in *Snow White*. Most of us worked at digging a trench to contain the blazes. Members of the Fire Department donned Indian packs, or "piss-pumps"—tanks of water they wore on their backs with hoses and nozzles through which they pumped a hissing stream onto the embers. It was hot work, and they were streaming with sweat in the afternoon sun. A couple of guys with three-wheelers were zipping up and down between the trees and refilling tanks from the reservoir.

By the time most of us got up to the Ledges, the main fire was out. But the flames were still roaring right below the rock, where the cliff dropped straight down toward the elementary school. And that's where the hard boys from the Green were doing their own work. There was a strip of oaks separated by just a few feet from the more continuously wooded face below, and just beginning to take flame in their upper branches. The young men lowered each other down on ropes to lop off the burning tops and prevent the fire from descending to the village. These skinny 20-year-olds in black jeans and white tee shirts, with their tattooed forearms and their faces that had rarely shown the town anything other than a scowl or snarl, were smiling and laughing as they swung through the smoke. Gripping the ropes with one hand and their keening chainsaws in the other, they dropped toward the fire and did the town's most dangerous work.

Eventually, the flames were all extinguished and mop-up operations were well in hand. At that point, I gave myself an honorable discharge and stumbled back down toward the village and bed. In my fatigue and in the darkness of those moonless woods, I somehow got off the trail and decided just to head downhill rather than casting back to find the place where I'd gone wrong. The slope was steep, my footing was uncertain, and I ended up sprawling flat on my face among the roots and leaf-litter. My glasses were knocked off and, though I patted the ground on all sides for twenty feet or so, I never found them. My hand did fall on my shovel, though, and I ended up making the rest of my myopic way down by grasping it upside down just below the blade and using the handle as a walking stick. As it turned out, I thumped downhill on the wrong side of the ridge, eventually ending up on Route 116. This long march gave me a chance to think about the remarkable service that nobody else in town could have done so well, if at all, offered by those exhilarated young men who usually got called, and probably called themselves, losers and punks. Watching them at work had helped me realize something that I should have gotten long before. Hanging around the Green, they had all been *waiting*. For the excitement, and the danger, that wars might have represented for their fathers and grandfathers. For the sense of purpose on behalf of their entire community that came with staving off this natural disaster. Finally, for something to do that made better use of their courage, imagination, and playfulness than the dead-end jobs awaiting high school dropouts in a rural area, and to which they would be drifting soon enough, whatever their sullen resistance while hanging out around the bandstand for a few years.

Losses enliven our sense of place. They tell the interwoven histories of a forest and a community. Danger made these young men feel alive, and useful, up in the mountains where adventures were still possible. After listless days when they felt left behind by the purposeful traffic of North Street, they remembered in swinging below the Ledges what it felt like to *play*. Our own three children aren't old enough to remember the fire of 1982, but this spot has meant play for them, too. It's been a place to throw rocks out over the tree tops and, from August on, to gather the blueberries that grow thickly in the charred soil just north of the Ledges. As a seven-year-old, Caleb liked to fill one hand with the small, wild berries, incomparably more flavorful than the plump ones we can buy in the supermarket. Then, carefully removing the twigs and the odd green ones, he would toss them into his mouth and crunch down on twenty minutes of picking in one enormous, unforgettable bite. We ventured up from a house that we never quite lost sight of below, to play the game of animals eating the seasons of our lives.

➤➤➤ "Directive" helps me bear in mind the ironic reversals and identifications that accompany escaping from "all this now" and rediscovering a sense of home. Those young men amid the fire found a renewed sense of vigor, climbing above the dead-end streets and stores. For them, it represented both an escape and a return. But separation from the village would have meant something quite different for families inhabiting isolated farms among these hills. More than halfway through his 62-line poem, Frost finally concludes his vigorous climb up the slope and settles in to imagine those who made themselves at home here, long before his own arrival. He must imagine them from the scantiest of traces, and his first tendril of sympathetic connection arrestingly links a farm's disappearance with the emotional lives of children.

> The only field
> Now left's no bigger than a harness gall.

To compare a field to the gall, or sore, caused on a farm animal by the rubbing of a harness, is essentially to say that it's completely gone—no larger than any other space among the trees. But it is also an image of labor so severe as to entail physical suffering, both for the horse whose haunches shook in drawing ancient roots and stones out of the ground and for the man who followed along cracking the heavy harness-straps and pulling with both hands as a stump was slowly pried up like an impacted molar. This is the blistered glimpse with which Frost begins to focus his imagination of another life in a more concrete way. A Vermont hill-farm might have seemed the quintessence of American Pastoral—a scene of Jeffersonian yeoman-farmers clearing a space for themselves in the green world, building their family's home in a round of healthy work, livestock, independence, new beginnings. As at the beginning of "Directive," though, the poem takes care to forestall nostalgia. The poet's, the speaker's, and the reader's efforts to make ourselves at home find an "earnest" precedent in the farmer's own heartbreaking days of work.

We don't remember, and love, the past because it was painless and perfect. We don't cherish our parents because they had it all right. Love grows with the growing recognition of perpetual brokenness. But it is also important to note that Frost shows us a *harness* gall. Work has been accomplished here, a home made. Eventual defeat, when there have been earnest efforts, is no failure. As Ring Lardner said, the odds in all life are 6 to 5 against—house odds. But Frost sees in earthly life far more a vale of soul-making than a fully equipped and indemnified life-care community. In the front of a Bible my parents gave me fifteen years ago, they inscribed Proverbs 14:4: "Where no oxen are the crib is clean, but there is much increase by the strength of the ox." Labor and loss bring their own gifts. The maple-saturated slope above Bristol flames in fall only because these fields were given to the sky. A forest is the culmination of this farm.

> First there's the children's house of make-believe,
> Some shattered dishes underneath a pine,
> The playthings in the playhouse of the children.

I'm often reminded, while ranging the Vermont woods, of the austere beauty of Japanese gardens and paintings. And these lines from "Directive" make me think of a Japanese Noh theater, which has as its backdrop a massive, wind-bent pine painted on an otherwise unadorned wooden wall. This is the tree of life enduring, presiding over the drama of love, betrayal, loyalty, longing, memory; over the skirl of flutes and the rattle of drums, the mysterious furling and unfurling of sleeves in that slow dance. After pausing at the vanished field, Frost points "first" to a playhouse underneath a pine. The children's make-believe is thus magnified into the framing drama of this familial landscape. But what does their play have to do with making *ourselves* at home among these hills?

Though Frost repeats, and thus emphasizes, the word "children" within his three-line sentence, I feel that the image is not to be taken at face value. The make-believe is his. These Vermont settlers, laboring at the edge of survival, would not have built a playhouse for their young ones. Children here would have had to imagine their place, perhaps under the green roof of a pine. And the shattered dishes juxtaposed with the overhanging boughs are the scraps from which the poet is able to imagine their imagining. While Marianne Moore described a poem as imaginary gardens with real toads in them, Frost shows us real children in an imagined playhouse.

Another link the poet establishes is between the words "shattered" and "play." Only when the dishes are broken will the children be allowed to play with them—just as the reduction of their whole family's life to fragments gives an onlooker scope to imagine how they and the whole of their life might be recomposed. After dreaded disasters, a new, more carefree approach to life becomes possible. "Unless ye become as little children, ye will never enter into the Kingdom of Heaven," Jesus says. "Come, let's away to prison," Lear says to Cordelia after his reign has been shattered. "We two alone will sing like birds i' th' cage." His mind has been crushed, as well as his power and dignity, but he has gained equanimity in stripping off his lendings and giving his body to the storm. In temporar-

ily rejoining his daughter, he finds the companion with whom he can experience shattering as an occasion for play.

Frost's first word in this sentence is "First." He starts out by imagining the children, then grows up to imagining the grown-ups. His approach to a vanished family and society is not deconstruction but reconstruction. Entering the playhouse is practice for entering "the house that is no more a house." His project is the recovery of lost time, through the parallels of seasons and generations, and in the mysterious unity suffusing the absence and difference of these recovered woods. Once more, Wordsworth sheds his reflective light on Frost's poem, in these lines from the conclusion of "Tintern Abbey":

> Nor perchance,
> If I should be, where I no more can hear
> Thy voice, nor catch from thy wild eyes these gleams
> Of past existence, wilt thou then forget
> That on the banks of this delightful stream
> We stood together; and that I, so long
> A worshipper of Nature, hither came,
> Unwearied in that service: rather say
> With warmer love, oh! with far deeper zeal
> Of holier love. Nor wilt thou then forget,
> That after many wanderings, many years
> Of absence, these steep woods and lofty cliffs,
> And this green pastoral landscape, were to me
> More dear, both for themselves, and for thy sake.

The reader and the long-ago farm family are both alone and together under the waning, waxing moon that climbs above the persistent pine.

Weep for what little things could make them glad.

This is one of several remarkably Shakespearean lines near the end of "Directive." On the level of sound alone it is extraordinary. A reversal of stresses in the first two syllables plants the imperative in our minds, while the consonance and assonance that follow, and the interplay of hard and soft sounds, make of the sentence a beautifully interwoven music. "Weep" and "glad" bracket the command like a riddle, or a rhyme. Are we supposed to weep for how little these children and their parents had, in pity for their impoverishment, failure, and displacement among these hills? Or might the weeping be for our own incapacity, in these consumer decades, to summon a similar joy of living? It may also be that weeping here is a celebration, of their success at making themselves at home with only shattered dishes underneath the pine.

Frost characterized his own wonderfully controlled ambiguity as "a certain enigmatic reserve." But this particular line from "Directive" has less to do with the poet's Yankee caginess than with mysteries beyond his ken and ours alike. Four years ago, I began to study and practice Zen at the newly opened Vermont Zen Center in Shelburne. At my first sesshin, or intensive retreat, struggling for hours with the koan Mu, I began to weep as I sat in zazen, until the front of my robe was soaked. Stumbling into dokusan I told the teacher about this, and she asked if I knew why I was crying. I shook my head, face wet with tears, and she said, "That's good. That's very good." The question is always, "What's happening?" And sometimes the answer is "Weeping for what little things could make them glad."

My picture of Frost's poem, and my history of these mountains, are certainly my own story at least as much as they are any outward tale. And thus I will report that, just as Wordsworth and Bashō speak to me among these lines, amid these hills, so too do I hear Virgil at this point in "Directive." As Aeneas looks at the painted wall on which the sufferings of his predecessors and comrades are shown, he utters the line "Lachrimae rerum sunt, mortalia mentem tangent" ("These are the tears of things, mortal matters that touch the mind"). Walking in the woods above Bristol, I remember my father, dead at the end of August, and my mother, trying to recover from major surgery even as she struggles to complete her own grieving process. My childhood sense of security in a home sponsored by those compassionate adults is gone forever, as is the simplicity of a life when our own children were small—as is, too, the farmstead indicated now only by its shattered dishes. Houses sink back into the earth, trees fall and molder into the soil. And out of the ground of all these past lives rise branches bearing, through the winter, buds of another spring. Soon, the woodland flowers will open by this trail, though their appearance too will only be a brief one before the new leaves thicken overhead and block out the flowers' sun for another summer. In greeting each season, we must also be prepared to say goodbye. *Lachrimae rerum,* weeping for little things.

Coltsfoot, Mourning Cloak

HOGBACK RIDGE
MAY 1 – MAY 25, 1995

> Your destination and your destiny's
> A brook that was the water of the house,
> Cold as a spring as yet so near its source,
> Too lofty and original to rage.
> (We know the valley streams that when aroused
> Will leave their tatters hung on barb and thorn.)

In all my previous years of hiking around Bristol, I have most often returned to South Mountain's Bristol Cliffs Wilderness Area, to the peregrine-encircled brow of Deer Leap, and to the Ledges above our village. There had seemed, from the topo map of North Mountain, to be few other features of special interest along this hogback ridge. Nevertheless, the present year's long-contemplated design finally drove me farther north, to finish walking the anticline while I completed my outdoor reflections on Frost's poem. I had few expectations for this stage of the hike, beyond the dogged satisfactions of effort and closure. The passage that I had arrived at in "Directive"—lines 49 through 54—seemed unlikely to connect with my trailside observations as closely as the earlier passages had done on previous hikes. I didn't anticipate that there would be any brooks on those stony heights, and looked only for hard walking through woods that held no particular destination. What I found, though, was that this hike, planned as one day's push along the ridge to Bristol Pond, exfoliated into a reiterated month of walking into spring, spring, spring.

Though the morning was clear and bright when I first headed up to the ridge, the wind was edged. The snow around our home had been gone for almost a month, but a sodden carpet of last year's leaves still adhered to the ground. Only a few of the twigs overhead had begun to unfold their buds. Still, as I walked up the trail toward the Ledges, with my eyes fixed on the ground before my feet, there they were—my first wildflowers of the season. Coltsfoot. Bright golden-yellow disks, looking at first like unusually tidy dandelions, with their slim, closely packed, and uniform-length rays. The coltsfoot flowers rose up through a layer of maple, beech, and oak leaves on fleshy, pinkish stems that showed, as yet, no leaves of their own. Scattered around them in the litter were tightly furled green spears thrusting up through the brown. These would soon be broadening and softening into the pliable leaves of trout lilies. But for now they maintained a pointed rigidity that allowed them to transfix tired old fragments of last fall, raising them off the ground into a less anaerobic existence.

As I knelt by the coltsfoot, I could suddenly hear the woods resounding with woodpeckers, as if they had been waiting for this signal. I looked up to see a hairy woodpecker on a nearby beech tree, working away with a rapid *rat-a-tat*. Invisible, but not too far away, a larger pileated woodpecker struck its lower, more reverberant *tock-tock-tock*. Two pert black-capped chickadees worked over a moribund yellow birch beside the trail. There was a cavity into which they took turns thrusting their whole bodies, emerging with beaks crammed full to overflowing with some chaffy stuff. They were waging a vigorous campaign to give that punky deadwood wings.

➤➤ Since Maple's death, I'd been reluctant to go into the woods again. But the camping trip with Rita up to the Ledges had broken the ice. Here I was, though still a little dazed, on a morning that simply was not going to let me miss the spring—even if, at the same time, it would never let me forget my griefs. It was to be the beginning of three and a half weeks of hiking back and forth on the same short stretch of trail, a period that redefined my entire year. Relinquishment of my expectations was the necessary first step. Easier said than done. But that was the necessity Frost, too, ventured into the woods to remind himself of daily. I've referred to his poem "In Hardwood Groves" in earlier excursions, and find myself returning to its final two stanzas as I think about grief and consolation.

> Before the leaves can mount again
> To fill the trees with another shade,
> They must go down past things coming up.
> They must go down into the dark decayed.
>
> They *must* be pierced by flowers and put
> Beneath the feet of dancing flowers.
> However it is in some other world
> I know that this is the way in ours.

When I read about the life of Frost, I resist focusing too much on the troubled and troubling aspects of the person behind the extraordinary poetry. I read these matters in the opposite direction. What a triumph it was for this grief-beset and difficult man to affirm in lucid verse the world's health and wholeness, while at the same time never scanting the confusions of our human condition. Frost could only accomplish such a personal alchemy because he ventured forth faithfully to encounter nature's news, and because he held his eye steadily on the changing surfaces of lives not his. Like his predecessor and model Thoreau, he dedicated himself to his "morning work." A reading that found nothing but birds and flowers in Frost would be a sentimental one, evading the irony, the suffering, and the mischief of his poems. But more academically fashionable readings that trace only suicidal longings in the poet's shady woods are no less reductive. Frost perceives familiar cycles in nature—akin to memory with its stubborn discouragements and its perennial consolations. Yet he also discovers, wherever he looks, things he's never seen before, designs out of alignment with his expectations. He mutters to himself, "They must go down, they must go down," as he scuffles through the old season's leaves. That's what he's sure of. When it comes to hope, though, he'll settle for uncertainty. It's enough for Frost to know that there are "things coming up."

As I continued north up the trail, through the cold, woodpecker-rattled air, a couple of butterflies flitted by in the opposite direction. They seemed to be of some drab color, with tattery, light wing-margins. But just a few steps farther I found another of these butterflies settled into a sunny patch amid the leaves, steadily pumping its wings up and down to get the circulation going. I could see, when I sat down to inspect it from a stump across the trail, that its main color was really a rich, purple brown. Each wing was decisively split in half, making the whole butterfly look like four wedge-shaped segments, or about half, of a chocolate meringue pie—sliced up and ready to serve. The wings' intricate edges were a pale yellow, highlighted by circles of iridescent blue that lay just beside them within the neighboring brown.

When I moved over for a closer inspection, the butterfly flitted off between the bare maples. But when I sat back down it soon returned to its spot, hoisted its wings straight up, and maintained that poised stillness even as I stood again and walked on. Only when I got home and looked it up in a field guide did I find out the name of this species. It was the mourning cloak, earliest butterfly of the New England spring—somber enough at first glance, but holding within its mourning-darkness the yellow of early wildflowers and the opalescence of standing water under a blustery sky.

I didn't walk on much farther past the mourning cloak before taking time out, as always, to survey Bristol from the Ledges. Whorls of last year's yellow grass framed, or were islanded by, sloping corrugations of stone. I sat down beside the old metal trash barrel, bright orange after the first spring rains, that had been sawn in half longitudinally and transported up here to serve as a barbecue. It was still filled with the pulverized coals of last summer's cookouts. Overhead, a hawk circled three times, its tail rust-orange in the sun, then sped off toward the east. As I rested on the rock, I heard a clamor to my west that I took at first for geese, then recognized as the Mountain Street schoolyard in full-throated play. A *tock-tock-tock* rose from North Street where one of our neighbors was out reshingling her roof.

> Your destination and your destiny's
> A brook that was the water of the house . . .

Although I had never imagined there would actually be a brook so near the highest ridge, I did not continue far past the Ledges before discovering that this would be a day of more surprises. Right after crossing a brushy rise in the trail, I was mobbed by the racket of peepers in a little pond. There were three different vocal parts in this choir—incessant, high-pitched *peeps,* an alto *quackety-quackety,* and an occasional basso *ribbet.* All those voices interwove into a single cantata, with "Love, love, love!" "No, over here! me!" and "Quick!" as the burdens of the song. All around the pond, too, there were woodpeckers chipping away in ecstasy, with a mountain of bright yellow chips at the base of one big beech to show where a pileated had just been plying its craft. Robins flitted about the lower branches, but silently, as if they felt their gorgeous voices were for once superfluous. The morning had begun in somber monochrome, but amid the sudden din a flock of thoughts and sensations flickered through my head and heart, never alighting for long. In his journal for May 14, 1838, Emerson coined the term "a Bird-while":

"In a natural chronometer, a Bird-while may be admitted as one of the metres, since the space most of the wild birds will allow you to make your observations on them when they alight near you in the woods, is a pretty equal and familiar measure." Bird-whiles had become the metronome, on this day, for the flights and perchings of my own sensations and associations.

I found that I was smiling as I moved on, even as the peepers' chorus died away behind my back. Then, just as the trail disappeared and right before the frogs were entirely out of hearing, I began to pick up a rustling sound in the leaves, looked to my left, and there it was—my destiny, a brook. It flowed in a rocky channel, and quickly enough to make a splash as it fell a foot or so over a little shelf. It was, as the last stanza of Frost's "Going for Water" describes,

> A note as from a single place,
> A slender tinkling fall that made
> Now drops that floated on the pool
> Like pearls, and now a silver blade.

I lingered beside that brook for the rest of the morning. It was scarcely two feet across at the widest, with brown leaves piled thickly on either side of the current as if some finger had traced a meandering line through the drifts. A boulder by the water backed and sheltered a little slope of black soil, recently freed from winter's cerements. Sprigs of round-leaved violets were already growing here, their yellow petals glowing against the dark green of sphagnum. I felt both rebuked for my lack of faith and released. Released from the strenuous intentions of the day, as well as from the long-contemplated design of my year, with its steady navigation from one end of the anticline, and the poem, to the other.

Like many Vermonters, I have too often libeled spring. Winter is the main fact of our year, and the deepest mystery. Summer is a pleasant interval of warm, dry days and gardens racing toward ripeness before first frost. Fall is the climax and the culmination, with leaves like bonfires and air like cider. Spring is often referred to wryly hereabouts as mud-season—several weeks when it's warm enough for snow to melt but still too cold for us human residents to venture forth in shirtsleeves. We tend to think that if you want fall there is no place in the world like Vermont, but if you want spring you might try North Carolina. Yet "Directive," like hiking Hogback Mountain, is about getting lost enough to find yourself. Where you think you're going is your destination, but your destiny is where you actually find yourself.

Because it is so brief and so intense, spring in Vermont, like the brooks along the heights, may escape notice. But I'm beginning to realize now that this is, by the same token, the season above all others that can help me practice presentness. I won't be open to it if I have to wait for warmth, or for leaves on the trees. Only beneath bare, winter-broken branches is there enough light for woodland flowers to spread their own leaves and to blossom. They must hasten toward germination, too, in a growing season even shorter than that with which our gardens' tomatoes contend. Every day for the first three weeks of May different flowers are coming in and out of bloom. Spring, like love, follows the vector of desire into the long suspense of unclocked presentness. This is no season for premeditated accomplishment. There is only holding fast while the world offers, for just a moment, the destiny of arrival beyond all destinations.

Spring rebreaks the broken ground and kicks over last year's leaves. Each of my excursions until now has been framed by "Directive," and has focused on a particular day among the mountains. But this day's discovery of the "brook that was the water of the house" both answered to and shattered my design. The wildflowers waylaid me. They brought me back day after day, as they unfolded with captivating, unexpected variety. I tarried, both giving up my timetable and finding other, more lyrical poems by Frost rush into "Directive"'s meditation on environmental history and its spiritual mean-

ing. If that poem had so far mapped my progress toward Bristol
Pond, my delay amid the flowers was sanctioned by the poet's
"Prayer in Spring," which begins

> Oh, give us pleasure in the flowers today;
> And give us not to think so far away
> As the uncertain harvest; keep us here
> All simply in the springing of the year.

and which ends

> For this is love and nothing else is love,
> The which it is reserved for God above
> To sanctify to what far ends He will,
> But which it only needs that we fulfill.

In following Frost through the landscape and over the seasons, the
brook of spring is where I finally lost my way, and where I finally
arrived.

Over the weeks following that day of coltsfoot, mourning
cloaks, and round-leafed violets, I walked up onto North Mountain
every chance I got. The peepers' pond occurred where a rivulet fed
into a beaver-walled impoundment, while at the ridge's height more
standing water welled up in a sphagnum-bog edged by laurel and
sundew. But the living brook, and the "water of the house," was the
highest flowing and deepest rooted of all these. It was not the run-
off from a single season's snowmelt, but the circulation of groundwater pulsing throughout the year, though sometimes hidden under snow. Even near the summit of Mansfield, Vermont's highest
mountain, groundwater wells out through fissures in the rock. Year
round, such a ridgeline tributary maintains a temperature of about
46 degrees Fahrenheit—which turns out to be very close to the

average annual temperature of Vermont itself. On the hottest day of summer and in the depths of winter's storms, the brook remains "lofty and original." It reflects the wholeness of the mountain and the year.

Linnaean naturalists frequently described the flowering world as a calendar, or as a clock. By this, they meant that when plants of different types come in and out of bloom, they indicate the progression of a season. Further, as blossoms of one particular species open and close each day, they register the passage of the sun across the sky. These early botanists also noticed that climbing to higher elevations is like turning the calendar back, since just a few hundred feet up the coming of spring can be considerably retarded. Over the several weeks during which I have hiked back and forth on this trail between the village and Bristol Pond, I have climbed through concentric circles of flora as if traversing the contour lines on a topo map. Starting on about May 20th, when the diversity of flowers seemed to reach its peak, the floral progression of my hikes up and down has been both predictable and continuous.

At the beginning and end of each hike, Canada mayflowers carpet the sun-splotched ground beside the trail. Single, sterile leaves shine among the fertile pairs of leaves that support delicate white spikes of flowers and give this plant its alternate name, wild lily-of-the-valley. White flowers seem in fact to predominate at these lower elevations of May. Starflower, with its whorl of glossy, pointed leaves, lifts up the stems of one or two little blossoms, each a burst of pointed petals like pure white miniatures of those surrounding leaves. Baneberries support their own sturdy, white racemes—with the longer stalks of baneberry blossoms promising white berries and the wider clusters red berries. This is also the week when bunchberries, or dwarf cornel, are opening their flowers down on the forest floor. The large white, sterile petals frame and call attention to the fertile, green-white flowers within their circle. The white flowers of wild strawberries are abundant now, too, along with those of look-alike goldthread—so called for the bright color of the rootstock running along just below the surface of the soil. I saw goldthread last summer in the Adirondacks, still blooming nearly at the end of July where the trail ascended high into the Range above Keene Valley. It had crossed the lake and climbed 2,000 feet higher to prolong its days of flowering.

As May has progressed in Vermont, other colors have gradually emerged to complement the white. Violets appear abundantly in the woods, in every shade of blue as well as the occasional yellow and white bunch. Greenish yellow bells are suspended above the clintonia's thick, smooth leaves. This plant is also called the bluebead lily in honor of the beautiful berries that linger into the summer long after those flowers have dropped off. In the final week of May, fringed polygala opens its petals, suffused with pink and mauve, at both the entrance and exit of this trail—signaling hikers to open their eyes and their hearts. I like the other common name of this flower, gaywings, and always think of a beauty-hungry farmer bestowing it as a lovename on this apparition that marks the end of a long winter.

Farther up toward the ridgeline, other flowers wait. All along the Ledges themselves, pale corydalis has sprouted to line the granite's cracks. Delicate pink and yellow blossoms with the asymmetrical, lipped form of a legume tremble under the wind of this exposed outcropping. The faint pink striations of painted trillium nestle under the oaks where the actual trail comes to an end, while the more sensual pink of lady's slippers glows in heart-stopping profusion under a stand of red pines growing near the drop-off. Indian cucumber, with its two whorls of pointed leaves, is an edible plant that the Abenaki storyteller Joseph Bruchac once pointed out to me. The flowers that hang down beneath the upper whorl are, like those of several other plants appearing at just this point in the season, a pale yellow tinged with green. Indian cucumber seems to be plentiful along this trail, so on a couple of these recent hikes I have dug up the white root of one, rinsed it off in the cap of my water bottle, and enjoyed its crunch and its fresh, delicate flavor. Sanicle, with its leaves so deeply cleft they almost seem divided, also grows here, and now shows its white-green blossoms. The other common name for this plant is snakeroot. Though I don't dig it up, I have seen botanical drawings that let me envision the long, limber root for which it is named.

These flowers of May encircle the heights like the ceremonial Shinto ropes we used to see tied around boulders and ancient trees in the mountains of Japan. The gaywings now emergent at either end of the hike have the entire mountain and its crowning groundwater surrounded. There are also certain moments along the trail where the whole season is bracketed by a couple of plants at a single spot. Right before the Ledges on my way up, I reach a place where a beaked hazelnut about as high as my head grows beside a witch hazel. My botanist buddy Alicia Daniel pointed out when she joined me for one hike up here recently that these two woody shrubs frame just about the entire growing season of our Vermont woods. The flowers of the hazelnut are among the very earliest to appear; then the plant holds onto its dramatically pointed capsule as the leaves catch up and unfold around it. But witch hazel, by contrast, will have the last, and among the most elegant, flowers to blossom on the trail, opening its slender yellow petals toward the very end of November.

A single flower along the way also can contain the whole ecosystem, and its seasons as well, if one has a chance to watch it through the circling years. One such plant for me is the false Solomon's seal. With its white flowers spraying forth in May from the tip of its large compound leaves, it is one of our most noticeable native wildflowers. But even more striking than its flowering stage is the way this plant's berries will progress through the summer. Early on, they will be creamy with dark speckles, suggesting the eggs of a tiny wild bird. As the woods grow warm and dusty in midsummer, the berries will turn blood-red. Because false Solomon's seal is plentiful in our range of the Green Mountains, a hiker in July is certain to encounter its terminal clusters of red day after day. Along with clintonia's dark blue berries and the delicate white flowers of the wood sorrel, this is one of the most colorful and long-lasting decorations of the trail. Then, in August, the berries drop off one by one (or are carried away) until just the stalks remain—like the stems of a grape-bunch picked clean. Every stage in this floral progression recalls all the others. Strong, dark leaves, laddered along the crooked stalk of a false Solomon's seal, climb toward high summer, and a single berry holds the summer's long fruition.

After the flowers of the false Solomon's seal have begun to drop but before the berries have yet formed, I finally make myself push on along this ridge to Bristol Pond. All winter, while pursuing these hikes, I have also been building the cedar-strip canoe in memory of my father, and have realized that its completion will coincide with the end of my hiking project and my book. After a winter of working beside the large kerosene heater in our drafty garage, I have now completed the Tribute's hull and am in the final stages of sanding it, out in the spring air of our backyard. Only the thwarts and the seats, the inscription, and the fiberglassing remain. I want to hit the water simultaneously with hike, poem, and canoe, to finish my projected twelfth and final chapter, then to paddle home and take a rest.

Still, having lolled along the trailless ridge for the past several weeks, I feel some reluctance about relinquishing the floral confusion to complete my long design. Though there is no actual path along these heights, the ridge itself is narrow and well defined. It rises and curves like an elevated walkway, or like the gravel flow of an esker that marks where an ancient river ran beneath glacial till. I have felt drowsy and warm in this stretch, not just because of the advancing season but also because of the thick tree cover that buffers me from the Ledges' wind. Painted trillium are common, as May draws to an end, and the striped maples are also in flower, with golden chains of blossom dangling from the twigs on their soft stems. Red-eyed vireos, the cheerleaders of these late-spring woods, call out incessantly in short bursts of song. The other notable birdsong, if you can call it that, comes from a nest of little hairy woodpeckers. I never see them, but they keep up a loud peeping chorus from the round hole in a tree where their mother has left them while pursuing more grubs to fill those beaks.

As I walk the rest of the way north, I have seen many low spots just to the west of my plateau. They contained the last vestiges of vernal pools—shallow depressions beneath the trees, nearly dried out now and papered with a coat of last year's bleached, beige leaves. These are the pools annually produced not by the brook but by snowmelt—nurseries both for spring wildflowers and for the spawn of frogs and salamanders, which are protected from devouring fish by the fact that there is no year-round aquatic access to such ephemeral bodies of water.

This has been an excursion in which I've been waylaid both by May's flowers and by Frost's lyrical poems of the season. "Spring Pools" has inevitably come to mind as I passed these little basins where water would have shone last week. Disappearing vernal pools have been my gauge, indicating that this season, and this chapter, were nearly over.

> These pools that, though in forests, still reflect
> The total sky almost without defect,
> And like the flowers beside them, chill and shiver,
> Will like the flowers beside them soon be gone,
> And yet not out by any brook or river,
> But up by roots to bring dark foliage on.
>
> The trees that have it in their pent-up buds
> To darken nature and be summer woods—

> Let them think twice before they use their powers
> To blot out and drink up and sweep away
> These flowery waters and these watery flowers
> From snow that melted only yesterday.

The pools on this final ridge of May were gone—just barely gone—blotted out, drunk up, and swept away. The long-drawn breath of spring was finally exhaled, and it was time for a lengthened stride, on toward the pond.

As I studied my topo map I saw what seemed to be a saddle of land opening down toward the water, so I turned northwest to see if I could find it. Soon, the sense of amplitude and security that had wrapped me on the ridge was left behind, as I bushwhacked through brambles and climbed boulders and trees for a better view. Old logging roads came once more into view, and called me down. I followed one gratefully for quite a while, but it ran north while the pond was now more to my west. So I headed off cross-country again and ended up crossing four different north-south logging roads on my scramble down the slope.

The last descent was steep and rugged. Sometimes I would come to the blue-green tops of hemlocks and, realizing that these trees were rooted far below me, would have to backtrack and search out a safer descent. I kept my eye out for the water, and did begin to see bright patches through the trees. The first of these were stands of paper birch gleaming among the evergreens, however, or freshly tilled fields rising up on the other side of Monkton Ridge Road. By now I'd also found and begun to follow a new brook, though. It gained velocity and broadened as the other rivulets and I fell in with its boisterous rush into the valley.

After Frost's own description of the "lofty and original" brook—maintaining its dignity and its temperature regardless of the comically extreme shifts in Vermont's weather—he draws what seems to be a derisive contrast with the watercourses below.

(We know the valley streams that when aroused
Will leave their tatters hung on barb and thorn.)

These are strange lines. They contribute, along with another paren-
thesis, to a mysterious and fragmentary feeling near the end of "Directive." In a way these lines are like Frost's earlier conundrum
about the house that is no more a house, upon the farm that is no
more a farm. What would the tatters of a stream be, anyway? I've
heard two explanations of this image that seem plausible on a literal
level. The first makes it out to be a scene from winter. The swiftest
streams remain exposed and flowing even when the season has tight-
ened its grip on the landscape. When their water swirls close beneath
branches weighed down by snow, or casts its spray upward at boulders set beside the bank, ranks of icicles form on the trees and trail
their tips into the ceaseless water.

Another image, associated with the spring floods, seems even
closer to the spirit of "Directive." When the heaviest snowpack
melts in March or April, swollen streams overflow the banks and
cover their boulders, crashing down toward Lake Champlain as fast
as they can possibly go. Even in our own day, post-thaw debris can
be left hanging in the trees ten or twenty feet from the normal channel of the stream—styrofoam cups, rubber sandals, shirts, caps. But
when the upper range of the Green Mountains was thickly planted
with farms, there would without a doubt have been even more human litter swept up annually in the torrents of spring and laced
among the trees. These lines from the poem make me imagine a broken harness dangling from a hemlock's bough. It rhymes, in a sense,
with the harness gall which Frost used to describe the tiny vestige of
a field beside his vanished farmhouse.

Clearings and logging roads, tatters and debris, effort and loss.
This descent from the loftiness of a ridgeline spring feels, both on
foot and in the verse, like a return to "all this now too much for
us"—not only to the relative messiness of "valley streams," but also

to the pressures of urgent, if self-prescribed, agendas. As I come closer to finishing my hike, finishing my reading of the poem, and wrapping up the writing of this book, I find an increased sense of complexity, rather than the longed-for resolution. Similarly, the poem itself seems to scatter and sputter near the end. The four coherent and self-contained lines about the destination and the destiny and the lofty brook are now followed by lines that contain two parenthetical insertions, one strangely tangled sentence, and a difficult reference to the Gospel of Mark. "Directive" has been in some sense a retreat, but now the reader is challenged to carry its insights and connections back into the fray.

Frost has been clear from the beginning, of course, that his would not be a pastoral vision "made simple by the loss / Of detail." The progress of his poem in this regard resembles that of all true spiritual quests. On the wall of our living room in Bristol hangs a woodcut version of the Ten Oxherding Pictures, which we purchased while on a sabbatical in Kyoto. These images from the folk tradition of Zen allegorically depict an individual searching for enlightenment. In the first panel a boy, who represents a monk at the start of his practice, ventures out into the woods to find the runaway ox (or water buffalo in our version) of his own Buddha-nature. In the second panel he spots the animal's tracks, while in the third he glimpses its rear end sticking out from behind a tree and in the fourth he throws a rope around its neck. The young student of Zen is getting somewhere now.

By the fifth panel, the boy is leading the docile ox, and in the sixth he actually starts riding on its back—playing his flute, since there is no longer any need for the control of a harness-rope. Because his Buddha-nature was never really outside the searcher himself, the image of the ox disappears from the remaining pictures. In the seventh there is simply a picture of the boy sitting in meditation beside a simple hut high in the mountains, while a full moon hangs in the sky above him. The eighth panel is entirely empty. The boy has finally climbed far enough up the path, it seems. He has become lost enough to find himself.

I have read that in earlier Chinese versions of the Oxherding Pictures, there were only eight images. Emptiness was the ultimate destination. But over the centuries, two more panels were added. The ninth depicts a simple natural scene, with a gnarled tree hanging its branches out over a brook near which birds and insects also fly. The boy is nowhere in evidence here, but in the tenth picture he returns. He is an old man now, chatting with a child who is selling him some food in the marketplace. Behind them loom the mountains of the earlier panels' quest. The boy of panel one has arrived back again at "all this now"—the present, with its getting and spending. But he is changed by all that he has seen on his trail among the heights.

I skidded on down the muddy slope southeast of Bristol Pond. The stream bed had gradually flattened as it coursed over stone terraces thick with brilliant star-moss and banked with ferns. Though I had arrived at the pond of my long intention, it was nothing like the body of water I knew, and had been counting on, from previous canoeing forays off Monkton Ridge Road to the west. The water here was clogged with cattails and swamp laurel, while the familiar *chirr* of the red-winged blackbirds was replaced, as the day drew to a close, by the oddly vocalized clucks and complaints of a gallinule. Once more, it seemed, I had gotten sidetracked from my destination in the woods—with my view blocked and my mood shifted by lives unaligned with my own plans. I left my expectations hung beside the stream, though, and gazed at this thick, eutrophic pond reddening from a sunset hidden in the western haze.

I finally turned and walked back toward the village on a muddy log road, encountering two new flowers while the gallinule was still in earshot. There had been no such floral surprises for several days now, as I'd combed the ridge of spring and watched the day-by-day progression of that blossoming contour map. But here was tooth-wort, or crinkleroot, with its four-petaled white flowers. I got down on my hands and knees to inspect this apparition with its small terminal cluster of flowers, its two stem leaves each divided into three lobed leaflets, and its similar basal leaves. My *Newcomb's* informed me that it was a member of the mustard family and that its "roots have a peppery taste." Close by was winter cress, or yellow rocket, another member of the mustard family. Its bright yellow flowers rose up in racemes growing almost two feet high along the rutted road. I consulted my guide and looked, then read again: "Basal leaves with two to eight smaller lobes; upper leaves egg-shaped or rounded, coarsely toothed, somewhat clasping. Pods narrow."

These flowers came as a surprise, just when I had the flora packed up in my journal and thought that spring was ready to edit and print. They were complicating tatters on my return beside the valley stream. They were vivid details, previously unaccounted for, like those relics on an old farmstead renewing the familial mystery for a hiker lost while reading in the woods.

The Stolen Goblet

BRISTOL POND
JUNE 17, 1995

> I have kept hidden in the instep arch
> Of an old cedar at the waterside
> A broken drinking goblet like the Grail
> Under a spell so the wrong ones can't find it,
> So can't get saved, as Saint Mark says they mustn't.
> (I stole the goblet from the children's playhouse.)

The rain has begun to fall as I step out of the kitchen door. Although the sun has not yet risen, the sky has become light enough for me to start my walk. Pulling up the hood of my poncho, I turn onto Devino Lane, head north on Mountain Street, then angle up Mountain Street Extension into the woods. I proceed past the Hanfs' house, at the end of a groomed gravel road, and continue on a rutted dirt track. This will probably be paved soon enough, since several new homes are presently being constructed out here. Somebody seems already to have moved into one of them, and a dog is barking at me. I move by quickly in order to avoid disturbing the family's rest any more than need be.

Even amid the trees, it's not hard to find good footing. There's been logging all along here, admitting the sky on either side and leaving a broad if sometimes gullied surface from the in-and-out of trucks. After not much more than forty minutes of striding along with my eyes on the gradually brightening ground, I arrive at the southeastern edge of Bristol Pond. There are a number of camps farther up the eastern side, but a substantial thicket of water willow has discouraged such building right here. Just before I reach the shore, I pass through a stately grove of beech and hemlock, leading to a group of three rugged cedars. Both at Bristol Pond and in "Directive," cedars like to linger at the water's edge. Behind me I hear the rush of watercourses descending from this steep face of the mountain, following many separate channels down the last rocky embankment to the pond. The rain is finally letting up, and the approaching sunrise lends its glow to the mist that hangs over the water and me. I climb out onto a cedar log that's propped above the surface by vestigial limbs leaning against the shallows, sit down, and pull back my hood to take a wider view of the morning.

So much has happened since I began to take this walk through "Directive," and the poem has offered unexpected illumination at many points. Yet I feel in a way as if I have come to the most perplexing moment. The lines I've reached now strike me as Frost's most enigmatic, just when you'd think he might ease off a bit toward the end. Furthermore, the special association between Bristol Pond and the original Abenaki people of Vermont focuses my attention on the most serious gap in his otherwise remarkable breadth of historical vision. This gap is a challenge for me, as I approach the end of my own long project and face the thicket of water willows, where neither walking nor canoeing would be possible. It's also a chance to cultivate a deeper sense of home, though. My guide did his job by getting me good and lost, but it's up to me to find myself in a history that includes the Abenakis who for so long made this pond their home.

➤➤➤ Abenaki is the collective name for a number of Native peoples in Vermont, New Hampshire, Quebec, and Maine. The "People of the Dawn"—so named because they could see the sunrise before anyone else on the continent—seem traditionally to have traveled in small bands during most of the year, occasionally gathering in larger numbers at the Long Houses. Fish and waterfowl were always important sources of food in this water-rich region, and some Abenaki groups like the Penobscot in Maine were the acknowledged masters of canoe building. But the Western Abenakis of Vermont have not remained as much in the public eye as those coastal bands. Only now is their story reemerging for most of us nonindigenous people in this state. Because I am not sure what would be the most fitting way to relate their narrative to my own, I have come to the waterside at dawn—their hour.

For most of this century, history books declared that Vermont had never provided a permanent home for any Indian tribes. Rather, it was held to be an in-between place—a hunting ground or battlefield for tribes from New York and upper New England. In retrospect, this was a truly strange thing to have claimed. The abundance of fresh water and game and the favorable contrast between our Vermont soils and those of our neighbors would obviously have made this a prime landscape for indigenous people.

The post-revolutionary history of Vermont looks much different from an Abenaki perspective. Ethan Allen and his brother Ira were among the land speculators who claimed these traditional territories without much of a qualm, at a time of rapid political reversals and a booming European population. As the historian Colin Calloway reports, some of the Abenakis chose to move north quietly, joining their St. Francis kin in Quebec. The important village of Missisquoi was largely abandoned. But a large number of Abenakis did remain in Vermont, traveling and camping in small groups. Over the years between the Revolution and the present, many Abenakis also intermarried with people of European stock and, from an outside view, blended into the French-Canadian, lumber-based economy of northern Vermont. At the beginning of the nineteenth century, the dominant expectation among many citizens all across the United

States was that Indians would simply become extinct, "yielding place to new." While larger groups, with federally designated status and their own reserved lands, remained conspicuous and led to the abandonment of such an opinion, the Western Abenakis did actually seem to disappear, in the eyes of outsiders at least.

In the 1970s, with the resurgence of the Native American movement nationwide and with highly publicized successes by tribal groups in Maine in reclaiming their traditional lands, the Abenakis of Vermont reasserted their own persistence in a place where history books had ignored them. Their claims were confirmed by the work of independent anthropologists and historians like William Haviland and Marjory Power, whose book *The Original Vermonters: Native Inhabitants Past and Present* appeared in 1981. On the first page of their introduction, they quote from a *Vermont Atlas and Gazetteer* that had come out as recently as 1978, to show how persistent and recent the denial of Vermont's Indian legacy has been:

> Prior to the coming of the Whiteman, the present state of Vermont was largely an uninhabited no-man's land. The entire area was a disputed hunting ground claimed by the Algonquin tribes of Indians, who resided in what now is Canada, and the powerful Iroquois federation, whose principal villages were in what is now New York State.

In fact, though, as *The Original Vermonters* documents, archaeological and linguistic evidence, as well as a variety of well-documented encounters between Abenakis and Europeans from the seventeenth century to the present, prove continual occupation of this region. Both well-established villages and seasonally determined cycles of migration by smaller family bands occurred in Vermont long before Champlain's voyages of discovery. When, in the 1970s, the Abenaki community around Swanton established a tribal council for "the St. Francis-Sokoki Band of the Abenaki Nation of Vermont," they were soon recognized and accepted by other Abenaki groups. And on Thanksgiving Day, 1976, the Democratic governor of Vermont, Thomas Salmon, issued a state proclamation officially recognizing their tribal status. His successor, the Republican governor Richard Snelling, rescinded that order in 1977, because of pressure, as Calloway reports, from "organized sport-fishing groups." Since then, the council and its chiefs have persisted in their efforts to gain federal recognition, and to assert their rights to pursue traditional fishing and hunting without state licensing and restriction.

Though the Abenakis largely dropped out of histories of Vermont until their reappearance in publications of the 1970s and 1980s, Munsill did acknowledge them in his own history of Bristol, written about 1860, and he specified their close association with Bristol Pond. This is one reason I've been thinking about the Abenakis as my own footsteps have approached the pond. Munsill begins his chapter entitled "Aborigines" by repeating two charges commonly made against Indians by his Yankee predecessors—that the men were lazy and let the women do all the farming, and that they were sneaky and cruel in combat. William Cronon in his book *Changes in the Land* notes the contempt with which English settlers in New England observed that Native men apparently did not participate in farming. They either did not notice the other men's organized hunting parties or viewed such pursuits as merely recreational.

As Munsill moves closer to home and to his own experience, though, this tone changes and his writing becomes more detailed and interesting.

It is not supposed that any of these cruelties have been perpetuated by any savage tribe of Indians within the bounds of Bristol. But there is strong evidence tending to prove that they have at some period of time made Bristol their temporary residence and hunting ground, if not a more permanent residence. For in many places when the first settlement comenced in Bristol in 1786 there was to be found small places having the appearance of having been cleared and afterwards grown up and covered with a second groth of timber, coarse grass and weeds, and other indications such as a profuse scattering of arow points, spear heads, chizzel, gouges, axes and pestles and some other relicks the use of which is unknown to us. These relics have been found in abundance scattered over the whole territory, especially the arrow points and spear heads, and occasionally the gouge and pestle; and in some particular locations have been found to appear the spot where there were a large quantity of the arrow points in an unfinished state, chips and fragments of the same kind of stone and some arrow points perfect, and of all sizes. There was such a place on the premises of the writer, in Bristol Village, where he has picked up and now has in his possession a large number of arrow points that are perfect, as well as those that are broken and partly finished, and a large quantity of broken fragments. These arrow points were picked up within a short distance of each other, that is, within twenty or twenty five feet of each other, and he has found many others within a short distance of that place when plowing and they are now constantly being found.

Munsill goes to some pains to catalogue the chipped stone points and tools. He carefully cites a certain geologically inclined Middlebury College graduate named Reverend C. F. Muzzy who confirmed that these points were produced from stone "found in this vicinity, either in situ or as erratic boulders." Such "relicks" are clearly of personal importance to Munsill, and he wants to prove that the people who made and used them lived in his own hometown. He further strengthens this connection by bringing the story right up into his lifetime.

In addition to these Indian relicks is other evidence such as the bones of their dead and buried. Something more than a year ago an Indian burying ground was discovered a short distance North of the North line of Bristol in the Town of Monkton near the north end of Bristol Pond, and some four or five skeletons found in a sand bank and to appearances, as the writer is informed, they were buried in a sitting posture. Something more than twenty years ago there were two or three families of Indians that come from the North and stopped a few weeks in the woods a little North of Bristol Village between the road and the Mountain East and among them was a verry old man who then called himself about ninety eight years of age, and who was quite inteligent and retained his memory verry well and could speake our language so as to make himself well understood, and while they were stopping there the writer with two of his neighbors Capt. Noble Munson and Abraham Gage Esq. took an opportunity to go and visit them and learn something of their history, habits and customs.

By Munsill's account, this visit would have taken place sometime in the late 1830s or early 1840s. He and his comrades apparently made more than one trip out to talk with this man, since they took some of the stone implements already described in this chapter to show him. Munsill is gratified that nothing their informant tells them contradicts his belief "that the stone was obtained near home." This friendly encounter between representatives of the first inhabitants of Bristol and those who would have been inclined in most other circumstances to describe their own parents and grandparents as the town's founders came to an abrupt end: "The old man was suddenly taken verry sick, and soon died in his tent while stopping near Bristol Village, and was buried in our burying ground at the foot of Stony Hill, so called. The Rev. Francis Whiting preached the funeral sermon and all the Indians in company with him, as well as a large congregation of our citizens, attended the funeral."

Shadowy motivations might be imputed by some to such a turnout by "a large congregation" from Bristol, among these a sense that they were symbolically putting their Indian predecessors underground—out of sight and out of mind. But to say that our attitudes toward ancestors, as toward parents, are complex is not to deny their more positive sides. And I choose to believe that this funeral may also possibly have been a sincere act of homage, of reconciliation, and of atonement—no less sincere if it was in certain other ways inadequate and confused. This may be, of course, an "illusion" of my own. For I identify with those early residents of my town who wanted both to honor their predecessors and to strike their own roots deeper into this new soil. Certainly, their efforts were no more overreaching than my own.

➤➤ After reading this chapter in Munsill's manuscript, I began to wonder if there was a stone in Greenwood Cemetery for this Abenaki man who was nearly one hundred years old when he died and was buried in Bristol about 160 years ago. I phoned Evelyn Dike, past president of our Bristol Historical Society, who referred me to Larry Giles, the director of Brown-McClay Funeral Home, as the man who had the maps of town burial plots. When I reached Larry, he said that his maps went back just to 1910 but that the town clerk's office might have earlier records. Shirley Emilo, down at Holley Hall, said that there were some earlier death records, if not burial records, but that they were all away at the moment being copied in order to preserve them. Carl Nelson, whom I called at Shirley's recommendation, told me that my story of the old Indian rang a bell but he couldn't be sure there was a stone. He did mention that the oldest grave sites were close to the road and just to either side of the large, central gate.

Since we moved to Bristol in 1979, I must have walked, run, biked, or driven past Greenwood Cemetery thousands of times. It draws the eye with its antique, spear-topped iron fence, its magnificent specimens of arborvitae growing on either side of the main gate, and its grassy lanes of graves vanishing into the dimness of the wooded site.

One of the few times I had actually entered the graveyard was when my neighbor Ezra Dike was buried several years ago. On several recent evenings, though, I've walked down to haunt the historical section of monuments, looking for some stone for the old Abenaki man. My route takes me by Lyon's Hardware, then on past the entrance to Mt. Abraham High School. The road drops steeply down Stony Hill at that point, and I scuffle along the weedy shoulders beside an abandoned gravel pit marking the shore of prehistoric Lake Vermont. Then the terrain abruptly levels out again, and I'm standing in front of Greenwood Cemetery's grand iron gate.

Although some of the earliest markers here are still clearly incised and legible, most have eroded badly, into the effaced "graveyard marble sculpture" of "Directive"'s beginning. Often, just the tracings of a few isolated letters or numerals emerge, as if glimpsed through a mist. On markers whose stone is of a slightly rougher texture, splotches of lichen heavily overlap the inscriptions, seeming to find their first purchase on the chiseled edges of those obscured cyphers. Quite a few stones in this section have been "broken off" as well, and subsequently propped against the stumps of trees or supported on sturdier monuments. The river of Bristol's history breaks over and rounds these rectangles that were intended to stand outside of time.

Most of the bodies here have long since transpired through the thick, sweet grass, as the stones themselves have yielded to the weather. I feel in walking here as if the grief of parents and widows has also gradually been liberated and dispersed. The memorial verse on one stone in this section reads, "We would have kept our child, / Which God in kindness lent / But e'er with sin defiled / Her life's short year was spent." The suffering of those parents speaks from the still uneffaced stone, as it also does from two small markers nearby that read simply "INFANT" and "Baby." But all of those parents have themselves been dead for a century and a half now. In the longer years of their lives, and in the fullness of time that has come after them, grief has matured and died a natural death of its own.

While I will never know for sure if that aged Abenaki man ever had a gravestone of his own, there are certainly many lichen-encrusted and absolutely indecipherable monuments to imagine as his. My wish to make such a connection reflects a desire to include him somehow in the family of this place where I am trying to make myself at home. The obvious irony is that none of my own ancestors are buried in Greenwood Cemetery. Our family is not native here. When Caleb and Matthew were both still at Mountain Street School, an informal playground debate was held over a period of several days about what constituted a native of Bristol. The judgment ultimately arrived at by consensus was a somewhat baroque yet interesting one: for a kid to call his or her family native required that all four grandparents either be living here still or be buried in a local cemetery. One can imagine all sorts of legalistic problems with this definition, involving old Vermonters retired in Florida or grandparents visiting from New Jersey who suddenly became mortally ill. Still, it is a powerful expression of the desire for family roots, and a sense of belonging, that reach deeper than one's own life. It is not so far removed from my impulse to scatter a portion of my father's ashes on the brow of Mt. Abraham, which looks down over Bristol.

I did come upon one impressive monument from just about the right period whose inscription was altogether clear. At the scalloped top of the stately stone page there was a stylized sunburst design, surmounting an incised picture of a weeping willow and an urn. Below, I read:

Robert Holley
Esq.
Who served his country in
the war of the revolution, 6 years 11 months; & was for some
time a sergent commanding Gen.
Lafayett's life guard, was a
prisoner on board the Jersey

prison Ship of N. Y. was
honerably discharged, he represen
ted this town in the General assem
bly 10 years, was in the battle of Plattsburg in 1814; was one of the
Electors from this State, who voted
for James Monrow President.
He was an acceptable member
of the Baptist church a long time.
died April 18, 1836 AE. 77
years

It was good to learn about the man for whom our Town Hall is named. And the antique feeling of this stately marker was enhanced by the fact that whoever carved that elegant script felt no need to mock up the lines in advance or bear down very hard on the spelling. Finally, though, its interest for me is historical, in the more detached sense. By contrast, in contemplating that old Indian man without a recorded name and in projecting his life and legend on those script-less, crumbling squares of stone, I can begin to identify myself much more personally with an ancestor in this land.

The only deciduous tree that survives on Mt. Abraham much above 2500 feet is the paper birch. In the cold and wind near the ridgeline, it can propagate itself by underground runners even when actual germination is prevented. Standing in this old cemetery under the shadow of Mt. Abe, I try to imagine a way for my family to be rooted here by following an invisible network of runners underground.

➽ I have kept hidden in the instep arch
Of an old cedar at the waterside
A broken drinking goblet like the Grail
Under a spell so the wrong ones can't find it,
So can't get saved, as Saint Mark says they mustn't.

All along the shoreline of Bristol Pond, near my log perch, I can see a scattering of large old white cedars—the same species known around here as arborvitae, and which grows beside the Greenwood Cemetery gates. This is one of the typical conifers of the northern spruce-fir association, often standing near the water and with its roots elevated and partially exposed. I've just been sitting here, as the light intensifies and the redwings chirr in the cattails to my north. But the cedars, to whose pronounced "instep arch" Frost points, seem to be slowly lifting their feet and stepping toward the water. In the cool morning, these trees seem mysterious and knowing, as the poet suggests. "Kept hidden" can mean that he has himself placed the goblet beneath the root, but can equally suggest that he has simply kept the secret of the *trees*. In this poem about the grace that can follow the collapse of all human designs, we must learn to keep the secrets we are given, and drink the water to which we're led.

The fact that the vessel beneath the root is broken echoes the pervasiveness of loss and gain throughout this long poem, and affirms the redemptive possibility within shared suffering. But "goblet" is a surprising word for any drinking container associated with a poor Vermont family in the nineteenth century. It makes me rethink those "shattered dishes underneath the pine," and wonder if the damaged household wares might have held a cracked teacup or glass—elevated now, just as the diction of the entire poem has been elevated as the poet moves toward closure. Like the mountain stream so near its source, "Directive" too has grown "lofty and original."

In contrast to Eliot's *Waste Land,* "Directive" has in general pursued a literal narrative, with its powerful religious themes only implicit. Here at the end, though, the poet calls attention to his own drift with a certain bluntness—almost, in these lines' interrupted rhythms, a gawkiness. Frost is pressing the issue now, like Prospero at the end of *The Tempest,* speaking directly to his audience in an epilogue as if the full meaning of the drama could no longer be conveyed by action and dialogue alone. Or maybe these lines are more like thespian Bottom's asides to his courtly audience at the end of *A Midsummer Night's Dream,* letting them in on his dramatic strategies through a ridiculous running commentary. I'm hitting all around here, and becoming a little scattered, like these lines themselves. The fact is that something quite surprising happens in the section of "Directive" that comes between the reverberant tones of "Too lofty and original to rage" and the last two, grandly Shakespearean, lines. As the analogies to the plays may suggest, Frost resorts to increasingly tricky stagecraft, including the use of comic relief, a sudden shifting of scenes, and the interweaving of parallel, superficially incongruous plots. A guide grown garrulous may serve to pull together many of the poem's themes. This versatile voice of many turns is like the broken goblet itself, a cast-off teacup suddenly elevated into the Grail.

Lately, I've been reading in a tattered old Bible that belonged to my father—a thirty-first birthday present from his own mother in 1949, when I was two. The back cover is all the way off by now, and the volume is held together by a rubber band when the Bible stands on my shelf. I search the Gospel to understand Frost's line "So can't get saved, as Saint Mark says they mustn't." The immediate context for this line is verses 3 through 12 of Mark, chapter 4.

3 Hearken: Behold, there went out a sower to sow:

4 And it came to pass, as he sowed, some fell by the way side, and the fowls of the air came and devoured it up.

5 And some fell on stony ground, where it had not much earth: and immediately it sprang up, because it had no depth of earth:

6 But when the sun was up, it was scorched; and because it had no root, it withered away.

7 And some fell among thorns, and the thorns grew up, and choked it, and it yielded no fruit.

8 And other fell on good ground, and did yield fruit that sprang up and increased; and brought forth some thirty, and some sixty, and some an hundred.

9 And he said unto them, He that hath ears to hear, let him hear.

10 And when he was alone, they that were about him with the twelve asked of him the parable.

11 And he said unto them, Unto you it is given to know the mystery of the kingdom of God; but unto them that are without, all things are done in parables;

12 That seeing they may see, and not perceive; and hearing they may hear, and not understand; lest at any time they should be converted, and their sins should be forgiven them.

The remarkable thing about this passage is, notwithstanding centuries of predestinarian theology that fastened on verses 11 and 12, how overt the meaning of the parable itself is. It has to do with the need for receptivity, and is conveyed through a concrete and accessible example. On several occasions in the Gospels, Jesus makes fun of his disciples' obtuseness, and his response to their question here feels affectionately sarcastic. Such an interpretation is supported by the fact that, following verse 12, he painstakingly explains the parable, point by point, in just the way that most listeners would already have understood it. His explanation culminates in three famous lines that directly contradict verses 11 and 12:

21 And he said to them, Is a candle brought to be put under a bushel, or under a bed? and not to be set on a candlestick?

22 For there is nothing hid, which shall not be manifested; neither was anything kept secret, but that it should come abroad.

23 If any man have ears to hear, let him hear.

As I read this wonderful passage in the Gospel of Mark, it seems to have much less to do with predestination or election than with the need to become receptive through listening and looking as well as thinking. This is certainly why Frost, too, takes us on a walk, and points to the glacial grooves in rocks, the overlapping stages of succession in a third-growth forest. The wholeness of our human community in nature is there to be seen, all around us, even in the midst of "all this now too much for us." I certainly don't mean to promote "Directive" into the fifth Gospel, but simply to affirm that, like the Parables of the Kingdom, this poem is concrete and direct—absolutely the opposite of hermetic. The mountains are the candlestick on which the poet sets his verse. As for the hearing and the seeing, that we must all do for ourselves. The intensity of our hunger to receive the seed, and of our capacity for being royally lost, will show what kind of soil we can lay down amid these bony heights. The challenge is to climb the trail and look around, to register every detail of the scrappy woods and experience the story of the landscape as a seamless and inclusive web. In Mark 4:40—the chapter's second to last verse—Jesus arises from sleep to calm the storm-torn sea and comfort his terrified disciples. "And he said unto them, Why are ye so fearful? how is it that ye have no faith?"

So, Frost's cryptic allusion promotes a meditation on faith; an opening of ears, without the fretful need for resolution on an analytical level; a walk through the woods alert in body as in mind. Reading a poem for its thicket of sounds and its ledges of association, not just for its thematic paths, is like getting lost enough to find ourselves while bushwhacking through the uplands. And the poem that contains the mountain may also be carried along inside a hiker's rucksack, in company with a water bottle and a topo map. Outside and inside. We enter a poem and vanish into the wilderness. Poetry, like faith, depends upon the substance of things hoped for and illuminates the evidence of things not seen.

🌾 (I stole the goblet from the children's playhouse.)

Why "stole," when no one was left to dispute possession with him? I think the poet is acknowledging the dubiousness of our handling others' relics, and attempting to make their stories our own. This sort of misappropriation is especially easy to recognize in people collecting arrowheads or other artifacts from the campsites and gravesites where they are found. Even at Frost's vestigial homestead up along the heights, though, there may have been a certain presumptuousness in making ourselves at home by another family's undefended hearth, drinking from those settlers' water supply with one of their own cups. It's important to be sensitive to this ambiguity, and this possibility for violation, particularly if one is inclined to sift through the past for stories. This doesn't necessarily mean an end to all such sifting, just an increase in reverence, irony, and tentativeness. For how else does one learn to become a person rooted in the land, how else does one nurture a family life in tune with the seasons, except by the stories and examples of those who preceded us in this place on earth?

Bristol Pond was one of the earliest and most consistent sites for Abenaki settlement. Archaeologists have found evidence of Paleoindians, who may have lived in Vermont as long as 10,000 years ago, at fewer than two dozen sites. Their most durable records are the fluted points and chips in places where people prepared their arrows and spears for the hunting season. In Bristol, two of these ancient relics were long points of the Clovis type, made from the gray quartzite that tumbles down the talus slope at Bristol Cliffs and crops out along the ridge running right above the pond itself. All of the very earliest sites in Vermont seem to have three features in common—nearby sources of "lithic materials" for making points, good fishing, and other animal foods available. This eastern side of Bristol Pond has been logged right down to the waterside, but one can still find scattered specimens of butternut and red oak, two of the best food trees. There are also still hickory here, with the bark on the oldest trees curling out in rigid curves like old car-springs, along with a yearly multitude of the staghorn sumac, raspberries, and blackberries which were other important sources of food.

Animals abound near Bristol Pond today, as they would have over the previous thousands of years. The combination of wide, shallow water, a major flyway, and a rapidly rising, steeply wooded ridge generates diversity of life. Duck hunters still come to their brushy blinds along this eastern, cattail-shrouded shore. Beavers ply these waters, and have done much to enlarge the northern extent of the pond within the last two decades. Deer imprint their delicately pointed twin ovals in the soft ground where cover comes close to water. This would have been an ideal place for a band of two or three small family groups to pause in its seasonal migrations and to stock up on food before the onset of winter, when it would gather with other bands in one of the larger villages. From imagining, and remembering, these lives, I begin to see my own family with fresh eyes—with this same Hogback ridge looming above our house, the same white-tails peering down through the trees at us in the dawn hours when we stir from sleep. How quickly the seasons of our lives together pass. It would clarify this fundamental truth if, like those ancient Abenakis, we learned to count the weeks by the flowering and seeding of plants, by the return and departure of familiar birds. When Canada geese call us out into the road twice each year, and lift our hearts into the circling skies, surely we come closest to our dimly glimpsed ancestors in Vermont.

Just as Bristol Pond yielded evidence of the earliest Indian groups, so too it held shards from the later groups. Abenakis of the Woodland period camped by these shores throughout the past thousand years, after pottery and basketry had developed to their highest level. Though their baskets themselves could not survive until the present, we can still read the delicacy of their braided sweet-grass work in the pottery surfaces on which they impressed those cords to lend a pleasing texture. From the curve and size of certain textured shards, archaeologists can infer a typical water vessel of 14 to 16 quarts in capacity. The shape of similar vessels that have been found nearly intact shows the sort of functional elegance that was also embodied in an Abenaki canoe. Such jars had a round body for maximum capacity, a narrow neck to guard against spilling, and a wider lip at the top for ease in pouring. They were apparently used for cooking as well as for storage, with heated rocks dropped into the water to boil food.

From the words of Frost's poem, I can envision a broken cup with which to drink in communion with him and his long-vanished farm family. From a fragment of an Abenaki water vessel depicted in another book, I can see the hands that scooped up red-brown clay along this Bristol shore, that coiled and molded its elegant, serviceable shape. I can see the sweet-grass, fine but tough, being braided into cord from which baskets were woven and against which the wet clay of a new pot was pressed to make it beautiful to eye and palm. These are all imaginings, but accessible through my shared humanity with these ancient families, and through the plants and grasses that still tremble in this morning breeze, the trees that still stand watch above this shore. I press the fragments of vanished lives against my mind, and lay them beside my heart. This page itself is the scrap of memory's passage through the resurgent woods and persistent waters of my Green Mountain home.

I've done my best to see old lives through the mist at Bristol Pond, but now the sun is overhead and it's time to walk back to the village. My right leg, bent beneath me on this log, is dead asleep but starts to tingle now as I stretch it out and knead it with my hands, working the calf and thigh like clay. Just as I prepare to rise I hear a distant croak. Two great blue herons are circling above the water, quite far up and only recognizable through their distinctive silhouettes—long bills, recurved necks, legs trailing straight back like some extraordinary tails. They call repeatedly, sounding almost like ravens, then turn off to the north and disappear from sight.

A Confusion of Waters

CONFLUENCE OF NEW HAVEN RIVER AND OTTER CREEK
JULY 14, 1995

Here are your waters and your watering place.
Drink and be whole again beyond confusion.

≫≫ Since beginning my hike through "Directive," I've kept checking my progress on the calendar and on the map. This is natural for any long-distance walker. Starting out from Georgia in the southern springtime, end-to-enders on the Appalachian Trail know just about when they want to hit the Carolinas and Pennsylvania; how much ground they'll need to cover each day if they are to arrive at Maine's Mt. Katahdin before the northern fall turns blustery. As they gain or lose a day—from inspired walking, or from a bad cold in worse weather—they continually recalibrate the schedule. But the shifting daily quotas always have them reaching Katahdin by October. They anticipate just how it will be when they draw near the end and break out the polypro and wool that they have been carrying for so long toward that last brisk stretch. For many weeks in advance, they've been imagining the final mountaintop's deep blue skies and listening for the whistles of its white-throated sparrows.

Though my own trek through "Directive" and along the Hogback Anticline doesn't compare in mileage with the Appalachian Trail, it has still taken me the better part of this year. And many's the time I've looked ahead to Bristol Pond as the culmination of my passage from fall through early summer. Just as the village of Bristol offered a place to pause between South Mountain and North

Mountain, so too the pond would mark the *end* of North Mountain and of my project. It would be where I finally strolled northwest out of the woods and followed the highway home. As the body of water closest to our house and the one where I most often go canoeing, it also promised a kind of closure for what had unexpectedly become my narrative of grief. All winter, as I worked on my canoe "Tribute" as a memorial to my father, I envisioned it floating on the reedy surface of Bristol Pond. I expected to sit in it and, rocked in the swells of a late afternoon breeze from the south, to reflect on the transitions—from farms to forests, lakes to marshes, and one generation to the next—that unify and renew our world.

Teachers of composition talk about a "recursive" process, in which writers continually circle back to the beginning as they work on a given essay, reformulating the thesis and revising the structure as new insights shape their thoughts. Reading and hiking around a familiar landscape have proven similarly recursive for me. The broken line about the "graveyard marble sculpture" at the beginning of "Directive" has begun, as I have circled, to reverberate with the "shattered dishes underneath the pine." In the same way, the line about getting "lost enough to find yourself" has come to seem a gloss of the poem's final words, "beyond confusion." At a certain stage of rereading, the whole poem seems available at every point. In my writing, too, I had long ago planned to conclude the book with that image of the Tribute on Bristol Pond. I knew just what it would be like when I arrived there, pushed out onto the water, and meditated on the poem's final two lines.

Blue flags, the wild iris that grow along the southeastern shore, would be just past their prime as I glided by in the Tribute. The woods would be dark and quiet a few yards in from that flowering muddy margin, with tall straight beeches and red maples dominating, but backed by a fringe of hemlocks and interspersed with mature yellow birch. I always do pause when canoeing past this parklike opening into the woods, to gaze deep into the shade. This is also the section of the pond's shoreline where I can watch kingfishers perch briefly on the sumacs that overhang the water nearby, cock their crested heads with leonine assurance, then swoop chattering over the water. In early summer, bright blue dragonflies skim the surface here too, sometimes flying individually and sometimes as mated pairs.

I would paddle the Tribute onward from this composition of shade and sunlit life, toward the southern reach of the pond with its thicket of swamp loosestrife, or water willow. As the canoe glided forward in my imagination, though, the calendar would always begin to blur. It would become a summer made simple, not by the loss of detail but rather by the merging of three warm months into a single excursion. Now it is August 19th, the anniversary of my father's death, and I imagine the surface blanketed with large yellow grains of pollen, floating toward fulfillment on the molecular motion of the pond. All of the pond plants are in full bloom, including the white and yellow water lilies, the water willow, and the laurel with their purple blossoms rising even in mid-pond. Over the water-willow thicket kites a female marsh hawk, or Northern Harrier, hanging and slicing through the wind that shakes the stiff-stemmed plants. I have actually only seen her once in my outings to Bristol Pond, but since then she has always wheeled above the thicket of my anticipation.

Between the blue flags and dragonflies of late June and the harrier and water lilies of August, all of the summer's other flowers and birds are also active in my mind's long afternoon on the water. Redwings chirr and a great blue heron flaps ponderously across the western shore, hanging forever above a bog where the snake-mouth and lady's slippers of June are juxtaposed with the blueberries and huckleberries of the season's end. Memory's harvest is promiscuous, like the bookshelf in my study that holds pictures of my parents on their fiftieth wedding anniversary, of my brother and me at ages nine and five, and of Rita and our children, fifteen years ago in Berkeley. They are all propped up in, and they all prop up, my present. Paddling home from this composite outing, as I enter the winding, fallopian waterway that leads through laurel and cattails to the landing, a great blue heron launches from a bend where I have often watched it do so, and a green heron flaps more quickly off from the snag where I have seen it only once. In imagining this final passage out of the pond, I always expect a wood duck to issue from the wooden nesting box erected for it in those reeds. But I have never spotted this bird yet, and so I never do.

I have anticipated this idyll on the pond as a way to follow "Directive" to its final words, "beyond confusion." After forging through rugged terrain and swirling through the seasons, this would be a time to sit still on the water, a centered moment in which all of the past year's vectors could be perceived within a single concentric design. But if "beyond confusion" are the two final words, "Directive"'s very last word remains simply "confusion." From the opening to the end, this is a poem that shoves itself and its reader off center, refusing the sentimentality of symmetry. Its design is the defeat of expectations. Becoming lost enough to find yourself is not a permanently achieved, and therefore trivial, resolution, like learning to ride a bicycle or tie one's shoes. Rather, it is a perpetual practice—like a daily walk, like playing music, or like prayer. It is a habit of surrendering to the concrete particulars of terrain. We read complex, and even baffling, poetry in order to discover meaning that constantly pulls us off the trail with the chords and bursts and tangles of its richness. We hike Frost's anticline in order to lose our way in the resurgent woods, and to recall that every hike includes a world of downed and standing trees, not just the path that straggles through them. Literature and the land redeem the broken present from the clarity of expectations. The world achieves amplitude, unaligned with the axis of vision and offering the promise that, as A. R. Ammons has written, "tomorrow a new walk will be a new walk."

➤➤➤ While I've been trying to finish this book and this hike, Rita and I have been working through a fractured year in the life of our family. Our difficulty communicating with Matthew has been a particular source of worry. So when, early in July, Matthew told me that he wanted us to take the Tribute through Otter Creek Gorge together, there was nothing on earth that would have made me say no.

There was also just about no one else to whom I would have said yes. The Tribute was the gleaming product of a whole winter of work beside the hissing kerosene heater in the barn. It meant a great deal to me—as a memorial to my father, as by far the most ambitious woodworking project I'd ever completed, and as a promise of reflective solitude on Bristol Pond. Besides, Addison County had recently been swamped with heavy rains. I knew that below the steep rock walls of Otter Creek Gorge the water would be exploding along over invisible rocks. My whitewater experience is minimal, and furthermore, I've never been particularly inclined to gain any more.

Matthew, on the other hand, did know something about running the rapids. A summer ago, as he began to move into his darker phase, we had sent him to a camp in Maine that specialized in wilderness canoeing. The last thing he said as we dropped him off for the month was, "I bet you hope this is going to change my attitude, don't you?" We did, and it didn't. But he learned a lot about paddling all the same, saw some wildlife, and got in great shape. This proposal was therefore a chance to acknowledge and enter Matthew's own area of expertise, even if I wasn't sure it was matched to the particular realities of our place and season. I hoped that when I said, "Sure, let's go!" he would be surprised by my failure to raise cautions or propose alternatives—my usual role from his perspective. It felt great to turn the governor off and, on this sunny Saturday, resolutely to ignore the little voice that was muttering, "This may not be such a smart idea."

I'd canoed through Otter Creek Gorge once before, in our old wide-bottomed fiberglass canoe. Even though the river was much lower for that fall outing, it was still a memorable rush, less like the skilled control implied by "running the rapids" than like a roller-coaster ride which, once seated in my craft, I had no power to direct and hoped only to endure. Now, years later, I couldn't even remember exactly where we put in for this piece of the river. We finally decided to launch from the parking lot of a longtime Addison County institution called the Dog Team Tavern. While taking the canoe off our van, we noticed that guests were collecting outside the dining room for a wedding reception. Grandparently couples were chatting on the lawn that sloped down to the Otter, while boys in white shirts and bow ties and girls in flowered dresses played on the swings and high-glider. Matthew and I skulked down the lawn with the Tribute in our grubbies and caps, while the matrimonial party looked on with benign curiosity.

We were in a hurry to get our craft on the water, and were feeling conspicuous under all those eyes. But it was a hard place to start, with large boulders crowding our side of a strong curve in the river. We finally clambered among them to a gravelly channel on the inner bend, slid into our tippy vessel, and pointed the bow downstream. This was the first sunny morning in several days, and the overhanging maples, cedars, and red pines were washed and glistening. We'd picked up a couple of sandwiches and iced teas at the Mobil in Bristol before starting. Matthew had eaten most of his lunch in the car, but I now pulled over to a shelf of rock out of sight of the Dog Team to eat my own, along with the economy-size bag of barbecue potato chips that I was indulging in from the same spirit of license that let me in for this outing in the first place. Kingfishers were chattering over the water and bank swallows were arcing around them. As we sat on a sloping outcrop of granite we heard a train whistle, and looked up to watch the train snake over a trestle far above our heads. I'd forgotten that Matthew didn't particularly care for barbecue chips when making my purchase and, by this time, had eaten most of that big bag myself. Between feeling glutted on chips and knowing that the actual gorge and rapids came right after the train's bridge, I was becoming decidedly uneasy.

We packed ourselves back in the canoe and shoved off into the current again, under the stolid eyes of several fishermen on nearby boulders, their lines pulled taut by the force of muddy green water. The river was narrower now and the pull of its current mightier with each stroke of our paddles. As we approached a new bend we began to hear a low, pounding roar. I knelt in the bottom of our slim, low-riding craft, trying to establish as much stability as I could before we turned the corner. Reviewing the highly detailed chapter on white-water strategy that I'd read last night in my *Complete Wilderness Paddler*, I realized suddenly this was all going to happen so fast that my strategy would be limited to keeping the bow pointing forward and hoping we didn't hit a big rock.

Given Matthew's greater experience with whitewater, we had decided he should be in the stern. This gave me an excellent view of the first portion of the gorge, in which our canoe was still actually above the water. The rapids seemed much higher and faster, and potentially more fatal, than those I'd seen in televised whitewater canoe and kayak competitions. It had apparently been possible for those competitors to read the locations of boulders from the mounds of water that foamed above them. But here it simply felt like an undifferentiated explosion of white, as if Moby Dick himself were bursting to the surface. There was absolutely no way I could figure out how to read the channel or steer a course. In fact I couldn't see more than a few feet ahead, couldn't make out either bank, and could just barely hear Matthew bellowing "Draw hard on the right!"

I could, however, feel the tremendous wallops as my gleaming memorial encountered some concrete details of this one real river on one particular day. And I could see, with the clarity of a dream, water washing straight over our high, arched prow. First, it pulsed

over the bow deck whenever we hit an especially mighty standing wave, bathing the inscription to my father so that it glowed in the mellow light suffusing our misty world within the gorge. Then, as the bow began to take on more weight and dipped, the current began to flow steadily in around my knees, as at the turning of a tide. Our canoe never did tilt, turn, or capsize as in the illustrations of the paddling guide. Instead, after the river had lowered us a bit more, it simply shoved us straight under with its foamy hand.

Watching us sink from my end of that parade was a serene, quiet, and, on the whole, interesting experience—like watching a freeway guardrail glide slowly toward me when I once sat in a hopelessly skidding vehicle. But as soon as we were in the drink, the world of speed and noise switched on again. The canoe, Matthew, and I were all bounced down through the rocks at an incredible rate. I remember thinking that it was a good idea to keep our heads up, so that we'd simply wash over the tops of those gray lurkers. I remember regarding our half-submerged canoe with a friendly and companionable feeling. It felt more like a comrade now, propelled along beside us, its cedar planking lovely in the swirl. I remember Matthew shouting and laughing, the first laughter I had heard from him in months, and I remember yelling back. Something pointless and silly like "Hold onto your paddle!" or "I'll meet you at the eddies." It felt great to be in the grip of that rushing water and, dangerous as the moment might have been, there wasn't a worry in my mind.

The river did begin to broaden and slow, but even after we found our footing and began to drag the Tribute toward shore, it was difficult to climb out. The upstream eddies were in fact really powerful, so much so that it was a challenge just to keep standing in the waist-deep water, much less to pull ourselves and the canoe out. When we finally managed to raise the Tribute high enough to empty all the water, the going became easier. We could hold onto the rails on either side, push off with our feet, and glide into the bank at an angle accommodating the eddies' force.

These remarkable eddies reflected not only the sudden broadening of Otter Creek after its frenzied tumult in the gorge but also the fact that we had just reached the confluence of the creek and the New Haven River. The New Haven pours its waters into the Otter placidly, and with a calming effect, here at River's Bend. After that, the combined streams proceed through Vergennes to connect up with the northward flow of Dead Creek before debouching into Lake Champlain. I sat on the muddy promontory where the Y of separation joined at the stem of convergence and watched Matthew steering the Tribute up and down the Otter's rapids. He skillfully read the eddies' backward pull and rode upstream with minimum paddling. Then, shielded from the main roar of waters by a rocky point, he carefully aligned the Tribute before thrusting out into the melee and flinging back downstream toward my paternal somnolence. He was wearing my red Gore-Tex hat with the broad black brim. It shone in the brightening afternoon sun, like the touch of red on the harness of the horses that organizes Constable's painting *The Hay-Wain*. This scene, like that one, felt like a happy moment of family and shared projects, under the Vermont sky. Matthew moved briskly, purposefully, and happily in the middle distance, as I lounged on the shore, heart calmly slowing, and never taking my eyes off him.

>>> This episode of foolishness and contentment on the river was the true culmination of my year's project and of my encounter with Frost's poem. Bristol Pond would have worked as a natural boundary for my traverse of the ridge behind our home. It too eventually flows—north through Pond Brook and west after that tributary joins with Lewis Creek—into Lake Champlain, our bioregion's heart. But Matthew's and my wild ride on Otter Creek finally made a more fitting way to find "the water of the house." For one thing, it was a roaring merger with the New Haven, our true river of home. This is the river that bounds Bristol Cliffs on the north, then sharp-

ens the V of Bristol Gap as it turns west between South and North Mountains and carves its channel hundreds of feet down below the plateau supporting Main Street. The New Haven, after all, accounts for the existence of a house like ours, and of a town like Bristol, below the Green Mountains' magnificent, depopulated heights. The two mountains framing our town could be seen, as I have seen them, as a northern path that culminates at Bristol Pond. But they can also be read to the west, the direction from which their waters trickle, merge, and pour into Lake Champlain. In canoeing through the Otter Creek Gorge with Matthew, my only motivation was to do something he wanted, without interposing my own cautions and reservations. But those rapids also turned out to be our access to participation in the larger flow. They kept me from completing the transect of my intention, tugging me instead back up the eddies of confusion and into a new adventure. I feel grateful for the grace of this disruption.

> Here are your waters and your watering place.
> Drink and be whole again beyond confusion.

In his final lines, Frost assumes the voice of a magician, or a priest. Having gotten his readers good and lost, then haunted us with the story of another family's failure, he triumphantly announces that we are at last "here." In this word, I also hear his opening's reiterated "Back." We have finally arrived, having bushwhacked our way through memory and association, back in the present. *Our* present—not some idealized rural idyll, yet still a moment that is adequate to our needs. This is the implied distinction in the second-to-last line. Frost's earlier description of "A brook that was the water of the house" gives way now to the present tense of "Here are your waters and your watering place." We come to a moment and a scene where, as the final line instructs us, we can at last "drink."

But before doing so, it's worth lingering a little longer on line 61. We can surely hold off a bit, after all, with the drink assured. "Waters" is a primal and sacramental word, but why does the poet follow it, and end this line, with "and your watering place"? On the surface, it feels like a wry allusion to those genteel spas and resorts to which, in his generation, the term "watering place" was applied. The superficial discrepancy between his hard-luck farm family and their spa-patronizing contemporaries in the novels of Edith Wharton and Henry James would have amused Frost. Both his social scene and his relationship with the reader are rougher and less gracious. "Try *this* if you want a watering place!"

But, as throughout "Directive," Frost's language also goes deeper, down into the living circulation of the earth. The mountain brook and Otter Creek both mark watering places—where the rising, falling, turning, carving constancy of current shows "water" to be not just a noun but also our most perpetually active verb. Intransitive, it rushes with no destination, completed at every standing wave within the gorge. Transitive, it waters the new shoots that make a landscape live. Riding the river, Matthew and I were pulled together into this watershed of grace.

Grace, as our ancestors affirmed, is ultimately what sustains every good thing in our lives. But it can neither be earned nor assured. It is the continual surprise of a gift for which we can only say *gratia,* "thanks." And the context for our gratitude is the equally constant disruption and confusion of our lives. "Drink and be whole again," the poet promises, lifting the broken cup that was cached beneath the cedar root. The word "again" builds upon the long sequence in the poem that connects "Back out of all this now" with "Here are your waters." Retreat becomes a prologue to arrival. Journeying, as Eliot said, becomes a way for us to return to the place we started "and know it for the first time."

Every word of Frost's last line deepens the meaning of his entire poem. It's both the final sentence and a ribbon of blue that rushes through "Directive"'s heart. As I've remarked before, its masterful cadence juxtaposing monosyllabic Anglo-Saxon with a concluding eddy of Latin also makes it one of several strikingly Shakespearean lines in this poem. "Drink," he intones, in elevating the cup. "Whole again," he promises, both acknowledging the turmoil and tatteredness through which we have arrived at this place and suggesting that wholeness is a temporary state, not a firmly achieved resolution. And then there is "beyond confusion."

As with "again," I hear in "beyond" both a celebration of a fortunate arrival and a recognition that such a moment comes again and again, because most of the time we are *not* beyond confusion. If the poem continued, the next line would thus perhaps be "Back *into* all this now too much for us." Most of the time, we live not beyond, but rather in the midst of, confusion. On the literal level, "confusion" is the perfect word for the place where Matthew and I dumped the Tribute—here at the rivers' confluence. It means a "pouring together," of waters, energies, perspectives—a bafflement of plenty. Only confusion makes possible a beyond. Only the cross-pollination of design and experience, loss and recovery, brings the new thing into view. It is always confusion that we drink.

➤➤ Almost two weeks have passed since we sank the Tribute and resurrected it. It is now nearly the end of July, and I am back in my Bristol study. Looking around the room with its mementos, books, and maps, I search for a way to shape and close this book that has swirled past my design. A variety of maps have guided me throughout. Next to the study door, a map of the northern half of the Green Mountain National Forest shows an enclosure drawn along the wooded heights from Rutland to Bristol. Most of it is green, though scattered white patches within the official boundaries show private inholdings. The shape of this portion of the National Forest is similar to Vermont's own shape on a map—a rectangle just slightly tilted and broadening gracefully toward the top. The map offers a big picture, within which nature and culture enclose one another, in contrast to the more polarized vision of the western wilderness movement. Pondering it also helps to connect other pairs of terms we have too often separated, like science and poetry, hiking and reading. Towns circle around the National Forest as its satellites, and highways flow toward it like tributaries.

The maps I've most often consulted in these hikes, though, are the topo maps for South Mountain and North Mountain, taped end to end beside my desk. These limn in greater detail the topography around my home—where two massive brows of rock confront each other at Bristol Gap, where the New Haven surges westward below Main Street, and where peregrine falcons wheel overhead. The green of Bristol Cliffs Wilderness butts up against the white of Hogback's privately held lands on these maps, while pale brown contour lines thicken and converge to show the equally precipitous shape of both. This map's scale is small enough to show North Street, with a tiny black square representing the house in which I sit and type these words. Bristol Pond, though in reality a brown and weedy place, focuses the upper sheet of the map as a graceful blue egg, dangling from the northerly blue thread of Pond Brook. This has been the most local and familial map, and the best guide for my own seasons on the trail. I can see on it the palisade guarded by red pines and adorned by lady's slippers where I regarded the distant Adirondacks. I can climb the elbowing contours that lead up to Fawn Leap, and look across at the fledgling falcons as they race with their native air. And then I can walk along on the spine of North Mountain, smelling the thawed and crumbling soil accumulated spring by spring atop those bony heights. Like the ancient Chinese literati who viewed their meditations on landscape paintings as walks into the mountains, I too can hike within this map—my teacher and my aid to memory.

On the east side of my study, beside the window, is one more map, this one of the Lake Champlain Drainage Basin. While the other maps begin with political boundaries, then draw in the natural features, this one ignores the division between Vermont and New York to evoke the wholeness of our bioregion. The watershed draining into Lake Champlain is bounded by the Green Mountains to the east and the Adirondack High Peaks to the west. Just as the larger-scale map of the Green Mountain National Forest placed our local hills and woods within the broader human context of our place, this drainage map reflects the encompassing geological history. Our New Haven River is just one spoke of the water wheel that turns around and flows into Lake Champlain. The lake too is finally just one tributary of the single watershed that is our earth. And when we're far enough from streetlights to see beyond the earth, we can sometimes glimpse a further ingathering—a Milky Way whose turning arms enfold our planet home.

When I first set out to walk the ridges above Bristol and make myself at home, I never anticipated the convulsions this year would bring to our family. The losses of Frost's farm family and the disappearances of whole communities among these mountains had engaged me on a more intellectual level. But the photographs on my study bookshelf map a story of grief that has colored my narrative of hiking and reading the heights. In the small portrait of my parents, they are dressed up as if for church, my mother with her signature pearl earrings and necklace, and wearing a navy blue dress. My father wears a dark suit, white shirt, and maroon tie. They are both smiling serenely into the camera. When this photo was taken, they were already retired but had not yet begun to experience any physical decline. Now my mother is recovering very slowly from an operation and my father is dead. Grieving doesn't seem to have an end. Yet there they are in the picture, wise and content, patiently waiting for me to comprehend the watershed within which they still circulate through my life.

An even older picture leans beside that one on the bookshelf. It was taken during a sabbatical in Berkeley fifteen years ago, and shows Rita and the children on the deck behind our rented house.

Rita's hair was jet-black and, although I can see the wedding ring on her finger, she looks just as I remember her from her junior year in college. Rachel's a four-year-old, with those pink-rimmed, coke-bottle-thick glasses that she used to wear. With both hands, she proudly holds out on display the little flowered skirt Rita had sewn for her. Rita's down on one knee holding up Caleb, who's wearing little sneakers with his overalls but is not yet at the point of standing by himself. Sitting in the center with his yellow turtleneck and with rainbow suspenders for his jeans, and looking remarkably like the trademark Dutch Boy of the paint company, is Matthew. Whereas my parents' picture was taken when they were about fifteen years older than Rita and I are now, this family portrait from Berkeley was taken just about that long *ago*. So the center of the whole familial array is now. In the midst of all this grief and confusion, "Here are your waters and your watering place."

Which swirls me back once more to "Directive," Frost's topo-graphic map of home. Reading it has been a way both to hike these mountains around our family's home and to tell the story of our own generations. The poet has shown me that wholeness beyond confusion comes through, and within, getting lost enough to find yourself. He has offered a series of maps, each of which has a spot in it for this moment in the life of our family. He has told a long story of geology and settlement within which our familial narrative is placed and magnified. He cautions me, even as I write the last page of this book, to resist the simplifying impulse of "Back out of all this now," and instead to flow back continually into the losses and the waters of this place.

Crickets chirr tentatively outside the study window, tuning up for the throbbing, late-August choruses that consummate the summer and conclude the singers' lives. Asters and goldenrod bloom along the unmowed roadsides of our town, while jewelweed and nettles intertwine in the weedy patch behind our barn. In another couple of months, we'll hear a distant calling and rush out into our driveway to watch flotillas of snow geese and Canada geese oaring southward with the turning year. They'll go right above that hogback ridge, reversing my whole northward trek within just a few minutes of their flight. My hike through "Directive" has helped me identify with the losses and recoveries, the migrations and returns, that are the living circulation of our family's place on earth.

NOTES

Page

24 Leslie Marmon Silko, "Landscape, History, and the Pueblo Imagination," in *The Norton Book of Nature Writing*, ed. Robert Finch and John Elder (New York: W. W. Norton, 1990), p. 888.

26 Ibid., pp. 887, 888.

35 H. N. Munsill, *Bristol, Vermont: The Early History* (Bristol, Vt.: Bristol Historical Society, n.d., p. 160.

37 Ibid., pp. 164, 165.

42 Wendell Berry, *Collected Poems, 1957–1982* (New York: North Point Press, 1984), p. 210.

43 Ibid., p. 211.

48 T. S. Eliot, *The Waste Land and Other Poems* (San Diego: Harcourt Brace Jovanovich, 1988), pp. 29–30.

50 Jeffrey Severson, "Evaluation of the Bristol Area Cheshire Formation . . . as a Potential National Natural Landmark." Prepared for National Park Service, U. S. Department of the Interior (Burlington: University of Vermont, Field Naturalist Program, 1987), p. 20.

52 John Muir, *The Mountains of California* (New York: Penguin Books, 1985), p. 12.

54 Barry Lopez, "Landscape and Narrative," in *Crossing Open Ground* (New York: Vintage Books, 1989), p. 68.

55 Franklin S. Harvey, *The Money Diggers* (Brattleboro, Vt.: Stephen Greene Press, 1970), p. 11.

57 Ibid., p. 19.

59 Ibid., p. 38.

79 Aldo Leopold, *A Sand County Almanac* (New York: Oxford University Press, 1987), pp. 3–4.

91 Lawrance Thompson, *Robert Frost: The Years of Triumph* (New York: Holt, Rinehart and Winston, 1970), pp. 716–731.

93 Lawrance Thompson, *Robert Frost: The Later Years* (New York: Holt, Rinehart and Winston, 1976), pp. 135, 155.

97   Gary Snyder, *The Practice of the Wild* (San Francisco: North Point Press, 1990), p. 136.

101   Joseph Brodsky, *On Grief and Reason* (New York: Farrar, Straus and Giroux, 1995), pp. 225–226.

102   D. H. Lawrence, *Study of Thomas Hardy,* in *Phoenix: The Posthumous Papers of D. H. Lawrence,* ed. Edward D. McDonald (New York: The Viking Press, 1936), p. 419.

119   William A. Haviland and Marjory W. Power, *The Original Vermonters: Native Inhabitants Past and Present* (Hanover, N.H.: University Press of New England, 1981), p. xv.

120   Muir, *Mountains of California,* p. 64.

122   Snyder, *Practice of the Wild,* p. 40.

123   Peter Marchand, "Waves in the Forest," *Natural History,* February 1995, p. 26.

124   Ibid., p. 32.

127   George Perkins Marsh, *Man and Nature,* ed. David Lowenthal (Cambridge, Mass.: Harvard University Press, 1965), pp. 187, 35.

145   Henry David Thoreau, *Walden,* in *Henry David Thoreau* (New York: The Library of America, 1985), p. 567.

162   Ralph Waldo Emerson and Henry David Thoreau, *Nature/Walking* (Boston: Beacon Press, 1991), p. 85.

204   Colin G. Calloway, *The Western Abenakis of Vermont, 1600–1800* (Norman: University of Oklahoma Press, 1990), p. 234.

205   Haviland and Power, *The Original Vermonters,* p. 1.

SELECTED READINGS

Within the narrative structure of *Reading the Mountains of Home*, I have focused on three main topics: the natural and human history of the Green Mountains around Bristol, Vermont; Frost's poem "Directive"; and the relationship between wilderness and a sense of place. The following list, for readers who would like to explore one or another of these areas in greater depth, includes a few of the works that have been helpful to me in the writing of this book.

The Natural and Human History of New England

Colin G. Calloway, *The Western Abenakis of Vermont, 1600–1800: War, Migration, and the Survival of an Indian People* (Norman: University of Oklahoma Press, 1990).
  A richly documented account by this influential historian of Abenaki life in Vermont.
William Cronon, *Changes in the Land: Indians, Colonists, and the Ecology of New England* (New York: Hill and Wang, 1983).
  A groundbreaking work of environmental history.
Kenneth W. Dike et al., *History of Bristol, Vermont, 1762–1980* (Bristol, Vt.: Outlook Club, 1980).
  Extends Bristol's history into the final quarter of the twentieth century.
William A. Haviland and Marjory W. Power, *The Original Vermonters: Native Inhabitants Past and Present* (Hanover, N.H.: University Press of New England, 1981).
  A synthesis of the historical and anthropological record produced as the Western Abenakis of Vermont were beginning a new phase of political activism.
Charles Johnson, *The Nature of Vermont: Introduction and Guide to a New England Environment* (Hanover, N.H.: University Press of New England, 1980).
  A clearly written survey of Vermont's physical environment.

Selected Readings

Peter J. Marchand, *North Woods: An Inside Look at the Nature of Forests in the Northeast* (Boston: Appalachian Mountain Club, 1987).
A discussion of northern forest communities and the ecological dynamics shaping them.

Carolyn Merchant, *Ecological Revolutions: Nature, Gender, and Science in New England* (Chapel Hill: University of North Carolina Press, 1989).
Reflections on New England's human ecology.

Charles T. Morrissey, *Vermont: A History* (New York: W. W. Norton, 1981).
Includes a good account of Vermont's dramatic early history of settlement, abandonment, and reforestation.

H. N. Munsill, *Bristol, Vermont: The Early History* (Bristol, Vt.: Bristol Historical Society, n.d.).
A history of Bristol from its founding to the mid-nineteenth century, including numerous tables and data as well as anecdotes from the author's family.

Lawrence Newcomb, *Newcomb's Wildflower Guide* (Boston: Little, Brown, 1977).
The most ingenious and useful of all field guides, beloved by amateur botanists and professionals alike. Its emphasis is on northeastern and north-central North America.

E. C. Pielou, *After the Ice Age: The Return of Life to Glaciated North America* (Chicago: University of Chicago Press, 1991).
An engaging narrative of forest succession and the restoration of biodiversity since the Wisconsin Glacier, and a book that accounts for many details in the New England landscape of today.

Chet Raymo and Maureen E. Raymo, *Written in Stone: A Geological History of the Northeastern United States* (Chester, Conn.: Globe Pequot Press, 1989).
A readable and informative geological history.

Victor R. Rolando, *200 Years of Soot and Sweat: The History and Archeology of Vermont's Iron, Charcoal, and Lime Industries* (Manchester, Vt.: Vermont Archaeological Society, 1992).
A comprehensive treatment of Vermont's early industrial history, and a guide to some of the most remarkable ruins in our woods.

Stephen C. Trombulak and Christopher McGrory Klyza, *Defining Vermont: A Natural and Cultural History* (Hanover, N.H.: University Press of New England, forthcoming).
A bioregional account that focuses on natural rather than political boundaries.

Tom Wessels, *Reading the Forested Landscape: A Natural History of New England* (Woodstock, Vt.: The Countryman Press, 1997).

A gifted teacher's introduction to the "disturbance histories" legible in New England's woods.

Robert Frost

Numerous editions of Frost's poetry have been printed, and the biographical and critical literature on the poet is vast. The selection below does no more than suggest a few books that are especially pertinent to *Reading the Mountains of Home.*

The Poetry of Robert Frost, ed. Edward Connery Lathem (New York: Holt, Rinehart and Winston, 1969).

Long the definitive edition of Frost, and the source of all the poems quoted in this book.

Robert Frost: Collected Poems, Prose, and Plays, ed. Richard Poirier and Mark Richardson (New York: The Library of America, 1995).

An important new edition of Frost, containing much writing that was previously unavailable.

Joseph Brodsky, *On Grief and Reason* (New York: Farrar, Straus and Giroux, 1995).

The title essay eloquently explores the darker element of Frost's poetic vision and achievement.

Reginald Cook, *Robert Frost: A Living Voice* (Amherst: University of Massachusetts Press, 1974).

A collection of essays about Frost by a professor at Middlebury and Bread Loaf who knew the poet well, combined with talks by Frost himself on topics including literature, religion, and the sense of place.

Andrew R. Marks, *Victor Reichert and Robert Frost: The Rabbi and the Poet* (Alton, N.H.: Andover Green, 1995).

A glimpse of Frost's long friendship with Rabbi Reichert.

Jeffrey Meyers, *Robert Frost: A Biography* (Boston: Houghton Mifflin, 1996).

Especially interesting for its treatment of Frost's later life, and of his relationships with people including Kay Morrison, Bernard De Voto, and Lawrance Thompson.

William H. Pritchard, *Frost: A Literary Life Reconsidered* (New York: Oxford University Press, 1984).

A corrective response to Lawrance Thompson's biography, emphasizing Frost's poetic achievements and the continuities within his artistic development.

Lawrance Thompson, *Robert Frost: The Early Years, 1874–1915* (New York: Holt, Rinehart and Winston, 1966); *Robert Frost: The Years of Triumph: 1915–1938* (New York: Holt, Rinehart and Winston, 1970); and, with R. H. Winnick, *Robert Frost: The Later Years, 1938–1963* (New York: Holt, Rinehart and Winston, 1976).
The authorized biography and still the most fully documented account of Frost's life and career. Though adopting a startlingly hostile tone toward his subject, Thompson also shows himself to be a perceptive reader of the poetry itself.

Topographical Writing

There is a deeply rooted tradition of books devoted to evoking in great detail the physical and cultural character of a beloved place. The contemporary literature of place is especially rich. In addition to the works cited in particular connections below, it includes such outstanding writers as Edward Abbey, Rick Bass, Wendell Berry, Sally Carrighar, Rachel Carson, Gretel Ehrlich, Robert Finch, William Least Heat-Moon, Edward Hoagland, Sue Hubbell, Aldo Leopold, Peter Matthiessen, John Hanson Mitchell, Gary Paul Nabhan, Richard Nelson, Sigurd Olsen, Robert Michael Pyle, and Wallace Stegner.

Annie Dillard, *Pilgrim at Tinker Creek* (New York: Harper and Row, 1974).
An ecstatic realization of place, in which the author's far-flung reading frames her observations and brings Virginia and the Arctic into intimate conversation.
Barry Lopez, "Landscape and Narrative," in *Crossing Open Ground* (New York: Vintage Books, 1989).
A rich speculation on the relationships between inner and outer landscapes.
George Perkins Marsh, *Man and Nature, or, Physical Geography as Modified by Human Action,* ed. David Lowenthal (Cambridge, Mass.: Harvard University Press, 1974).
A book, called "the fountainhead of the environmental movement" by Lewis Mumford, that grew in part from the author's childhood in the deforested landscape around Woodstock, Vermont. Originally published in 1864.

Scott Russell Sanders, *Staying Put: Making a Home in a Restless World* (Boston: Beacon Press, 1993).

Eloquent meditations on the possibility and meaning of groundedness in contemporary life.

Leslie Marmon Silko, "Landscape, History, and the Pueblo Imagination," in *The Norton Book of Nature Writing*, ed. Robert Finch and John Elder (New York: W. W. Norton, 1990).

An often reprinted, landmark essay, offering a Pueblo vision of landscape and culture that connects geological formations, maps, and stories, and challenges western ideas of wilderness.

Gary Snyder, *The Practice of the Wild* (San Francisco: North Point Press, 1990).

Essays that take a bioregional approach to history, literature, and the sense of place. Snyder writes discerningly about the continuity between ancient cultures of Asia and North America.

Henry David Thoreau, *Walden*, in *Thoreau*, ed. Robert F. Sayre (New York: The Library of America, 1985).

Originally published in 1854, *Walden* has been a central and enduring inspiration for America's literature of place.

Gilbert White, *The Natural History of Selborne*, ed. Richard Mabey (New York: Penguin Books, 1977).

This book, first published in 1788–89, combined scientific inquiries with personal narratives in a way that influenced such figures as Darwin and Thoreau.

Terry Tempest Williams, *Refuge: An Unnatural History of Family and Place* (New York: Vintage Books, 1992).

Remarkable both for its parallel narration of suffering and change in Williams's Utah landscape and in her family and for its creative effort of grieving.

Ann Zwinger, *Beyond the Aspen Grove* (New York: Random House, 1970).

An account of how family life and attentiveness to the natural history of one particular landscape became mutually enriching for the author.

Acknowledgments

I would like to express my deep gratitude to the following people.

Lucy Harding and Ray Coish introduced me to the geology of Bristol Cliffs and explained its connection with the broader geological story of our region. Tom Wessels turned my eyes toward the "disturbance histories" shaping New England's forests. Alicia Daniel shared her knowledge of botany, and especially of wildflowers, during a sequence of memorable hikes. John Moody, Sam McKinnon, and Joseph Bruchac helped me become more aware of Vermont's rich Abenakai heritage. Any mistakes that may remain in the natural and human history here are of course my own, and do not reflect on the expertise of these gifted teachers.

A number of individuals generously read and commented on this book or portions of it. Chris Bohjalian, Lawrence Buell, Alexandra Christy, Alicia Daniel, Stephanie Kaza, Chris McGrory Klyza, Scott McLean, Chris Merrill, Jay Parini, John Tallmadge, and Deanne Urmy did much to help me shape this experiment in outdoor reading. I would especially like to acknowledge the sustained interest of Jefferson Hunter and Scott Russell Sanders, whose faith in the project kept me going and whose comments were always illuminating.

The editors at Harvard University Press have been wonderfully encouraging and constructive. My sincere thanks go to Lindsay Waters, Mary Ellen Geer, and Kimberly Steere for their help in so many areas. Portions of several chapters were previously published in *Orion, Vermont Life, Wild Earth,* and *Writing Nature.* I wish to convey my appreciation to the respective editors, Aina Niemala,

Tom Slayton, John Davis, and Parker Huber. The nineteenth-century engraving of the hills around Bristol previously appeared in *History of Bristol, Vermont, 1762–1980,* published by our town's Outlook Club.

My wife Rita has been my companion throughout the seasons and excursions related here. Whether discussing Frost's poetry, hiking on the Bristol Ledges with me, or offering suggestions about the structure of my manuscript, she has enriched the conversation of these familial mountains. "Never again would birds' song be the same."

I would also like to thank the following publishers.

Quotations from "Directive," "Two Look at Two," "One Step Backward Taken," "Something for Hope," "In Hardwood Groves," "Stopping by Woods on a Snowy Evening," "Going for Water," "Prayer in Spring," and "Spring Pools" by Robert Frost are reprinted from *The Poetry of Robert Frost,* edited by Edward Connery Lathem. Copyright 1923, 1928, 1936, 1951 by Robert Frost, © 1964, 1975 by Lesley Frost Ballantine, copyright 1923, © 1969 by Henry Holt & Co., Inc. Reprinted by permission of Henry Holt & Co., Inc., and Jonathan Cape Ltd.

The quotation from W. B. Yeats's "The Second Coming" is reprinted with the permission of Simon & Schuster from *The Collected Works of W. B. Yeats,* vol. 1, *The Poems,* rev. and ed. Richard J. Finneran. Copyright © 1924 by Macmillan Publishing Company, renewed 1952 by Bertha Georgie Yeats. Permission to reprint this excerpt was also granted by A. P. Watt Ltd on behalf of Michael Yeats.

Excerpts from "The Way of Pain" by Wendell Berry are from *The Collected Poems, 1957–1982.* Copyright © 1985 by Wendell Berry. Reprinted by permission of North Point Press, a division of Farrar, Straus and Giroux, Inc.

Material from *A Sand County Almanac* by Aldo Leopold (New York: Oxford University Press, 1987) is reprinted by permission of Oxford University Press.

Excerpts from "Landscape, History, and the Pueblo Imagination" by Leslie Marmon Silko are taken from *The Nature Reader,* edited by Daniel Halpern and Dan Frank, copyright © 1996 by Daniel Halpern and Dan Frank, published by The Ecco Press in 1996. Reprinted by permission of the publisher.

Excerpts from "On Grief and Reason" are reprinted from *On Grief and Reason* by Joseph Brodsky. Copyright © 1995 by Joseph Brodsky. Reprinted by permission of Farrar, Straus and Giroux, Inc.

Material from *The Practice of the Wild* by Gary Snyder (San Francisco: North Point Press, 1990) is reprinted by permission of the author.

Material from "Waves in the Forest" by Peter J. Marchand is reprinted with permission from *Natural History* (February 1995), copyright by the American Museum of Natural History, 1995.

Portions of *Bristol, Vermont: The Early History* by H. N. Munsill are reprinted by permission of the Bristol Historical Society.

Index

Frost, Robert *(continued)*
Backward Taken," 92, 93; "A
Prayer in Spring," 191; *Steeple Bush*,
92, 93; "Something for Hope," 93,
125; "Spring Pools," 197; "Stopping by Woods on a Snowy Evening," 138; "Two Look at Two,"
72, 73; "The Vanishing Red," 119;
"West-Running Brook," 2, 104
Fuertes, Louis Agassiz, 164, 165

Gates of the Arctic National
Monument, 20, 81
Geology: geological epochs, 50;
Cheshire Formation, 49; Dunham
Formation, 50; Hogback Anticline,
51, 116, 133; Lake Vermont, 51,
144; Pangaea, 49; Wisconsin gla-
cier, 12, 46, 49, 143, 145
George III, 34
Glacier National Park, 20, 81
Go, game of, 82, 83
Grahame, Kenneth, *The Wind in the
Willows*, 53
Grasmere, 33

Harding, Lucy, 49
Harvey, Franklin, 55
Haviland, William, and Marjorie
Power, *The Original Vermonters*,
119, 205
Hoagland, Edward, 66
Holocaust, concept of, 66

James, Henry, 232
Jeffords, James, Rep., 114
Job, 91
Joyce, James, *Ulysses*, 31

Kessler, George, 100

Lake Champlain, 71, 168
Lardner, Ring, 177

Lascaux, 38
Leahy, Patrick, Sen., 114
Leopold, Aldo, *A Sand County
Almanac*, 79
Lewis, C. S., *The Chronicles of
Narnia*, 53
Long Trail, 65
Lopez, Barry, "Landscape and
Narrative," 54, 67

Marchand, Peter, "Waves in the
Forest," 123
Mark, Gospel of, 215–216
Marsh, George Perkins, 126, 162;
Man and Nature, 126, 127
McKibben, Bill, 19
Merino sheep, 14
"Money-Diggings," 54, passim
Moore, Marianne, 32, 178
Morrison, Kay, 90
Morrison, Theodore, 90
Mosher, Howard Frank, *Where the
Rivers Run North*, 134
Mount Abraham, 65, passim
Mount Mansfield, 191
Mount Tom, 126
Muir, John, 22, 120, 121
Muir Woods, 99, 120, 121
Mumford, Lewis, 127
Munsill, Harvey, 34; *Munsill Papers*,
34, 35–37, 40, 41

Newcomb's Wildflower Guide, 68, 201
New Yorker, The, 153
Noh Theatre, Japanese, 178
Northeast Kingdom, 169

Oxherding Pictures, Ten, 199, 200

Parables of the Kingdom, 217
Pastoral, literary tradition of, 16, 17,
177
Paul, Saint, 110

Harvard University Press is a member of Green Press Initiative (greenpressinitiative.org), a nonprofit organization working to help publishers and printers increase their use of recycled paper and decrease their use of fiber derived from endangered forests.

15655405R00154

Made in the USA
Lexington, KY
09 June 2012